Judge Me
Dear Reader

Judge Me Dear Reader

Emma Smith tells her own story
as seen by

Erwin E. Wirkus

RANDALL PUBLISHERS

Thirteenth Printing February 1987

ISBN 0-934126-01-1

Artwork by Fernando Guzman
Cover photograph by Jamie S. Beers

RANDALL BOOK CO.
Salt Lake City, Utah

Printed in the United States of America

Salt Lake City, Utah

*Dedicated
to my
Celestial Family*

Table of Contents

Introduction   ix
Preface   xii

How it all began   13
Joseph commences the work   17
Harmony, our first home   19
On to Ohio   27
From Kirtland to Missouri   31
Joseph's incarceration   33
Building the "City Beautiful"   38
Family sickness and sorrow   41
The Missourian menace   44
Celestial marriage   46
The Mansion House, a splendid time   49
The Martyrdom   54
Life in Nauvoo without Joseph   59
Major Lewis Bidamon   64
Mother Lucy passes on   66
Our children grow up   67
Memories   70

Epilog   74
Appendices   78
Acknowledgements   85

Introduction

It has always seemed to me that there is more said and written against Emma Smith, the wife of the Prophet Joseph Smith, than in her favor. I am fully aware of the fact that, had Emma remained as faithful as Mary Fielding Smith, the wife of Hyrum Smith, many hundreds of their descendants would, perhaps, have been in the Church of Jesus Christ of Latter-Day Saints today and the Re-Organized Church of Jesus Christ of Latter-Day Saints might never have been organized.

I know that Emma (during the thirty-five years that she lived after the death of Joseph) told many falsehoods and brought much persecution against the church her husband founded under the direction of heaven.

As I search the pages of history I find few women who were asked to go through as much hardship, heartache, and tragedy as did Emma Smith. Emma completely sustained her husband as they went through one inhuman experience after another. Never do I find where she wanted to call it "quits", nor do I find where Joseph was critical of her. On the contrary, they were unusually close.

Someone said that Joseph had said that he would go to the very bottom of hell for his dear Emma. It is reported that when Brigham Young heard that statement he remarked that that was exactly where he would have to go to find her.

For some time I was offended by Brigham's statement until I was reminded by the great prophet Alma in the Book of Mormon that we carry our same thoughts with us into the world of the spirits called Paradise and Spirit Prison after our death here. There we will have a "bright recollection of all of our guilt."

Brigham Young was absolutely correct in his statement because Joseph would find her in the "hell" that she had created for herself and I firmly believe that, because of his love for her, he would redeem her from that state.

I have real sympathy for Emma, and see her "burned-out" mentally and therefore spiritually. I believe that she suffered a severe mental breakdown when she saw her dead husband. We must also remember that she asked Joseph to come back to Nauvoo even though he had said that if he were to return and stand another trial he would be killed or "he was not a prophet of God."

Whatever it was, we find a *completely different* Emma after the martyrdom. *I have attempted to tell her story as I believe she would have told it.*

Judge Me
Dear Reader

Preface

Someone said that Joseph had said that he would "go the very bottom of hell" for me. I heard that Brigham, upon hearing that statement had said, "That's where he will have to go to get her."

Of course, what Brigham reportedly said hurt me. I know that I did create a hell for myself and for my family after my dear Joseph was killed. I can't really explain my feelings. I have never been able to talk to anyone about them. I know that after I lost Joseph everything I did was a direct opposite to what my life had been with him. Yes, I lived in hell, and no doubt these feelings will follow me through the veil of death.

Joseph understood life after death. He will understand. Oh, I pray that he will take me by the hand again and lead me to his side.

I suppose that I will be severely judged by many, particularly the "Utah Mormons". And perhaps I ought to be. I would, however, like to tell you my story. As you search through it, please see that I did try to support my husband through all of our many trials, inhuman persecutions, and hardships; and I did do the best I could to take care of Mother Lucy until the day when she went to her reward.

As you search through my story, see if you can find where my heart became cold, bitter, died, and turned to stone . . . as so many have said. Judge me, dear reader, judge if you can.

Emma

How it all began

My parents were Isaac and Elizabeth Hale. I had six brothers and two sisters. My father was quite a man . . . religious, industrious, and an all around very good man. He was an excellent hunter and always had a pelt house full of hides for sale or trade. Father had cleared a number of acres of land and provided a rather comfortable living for our large family. Of course, mother helped a lot too; supplementing the family income by taking in boarders, providing meals and lodging for the people who were traveling through. A part of our house actually became a regular inn or tavern as it was called in those days.

It was because of the tavern that I met my wonderful husband, Joseph Smith. You see, Joseph was hired by Josiah Stoal, a friend of ours, to come and work for him. Since Mr. Stoal did not have any place to board Joseph, mother provided room and board for him. Josiah got himself involved in a kind of a "dream mine" project. You see, "it was rumored that long, long ago some Spanish pirates visited the region round about Harmony, and extracted from the soil an immense amount of silver ore; taking some of it with them, they buried the rest deep in the earth and left, never again to return." As I said, Josiah had some dreams about his mine, and therefore hired some men, Joseph among them, to help find the silver. As I recall, Joseph was involved with this "adventure" for about a month.

I thought that Josiah had hired Joseph to work for him because Joseph was so strong and well built. I soon learned, however, that Josiah had heard a little about the visions Joseph had had and wanted to exploit this gift if he could.

Strange how Joseph's experiences in up-state New York had filtered all the way down here to Harmony. The only trouble was that each time a story was retold it was embellished until there was hardly a word of truth in what was being said. Joseph was teased, cursed or made fun of nearly everywhere he went. I could feel his hurt and could see that he was the happiest when he was alone or when just the two of us were together. I am sure that he could feel the special sympathy, or perhaps it was love, that I had for him that early in our acquaintance.

My father and mother and all of my brothers and sisters chose to believe the evil things that were said about Joseph instead of taking the time to learn what was in his heart. I could not blame them, however, because there were so many vicious things being said and it is only human nature to judge without truly getting to know him. I will have to admit that in the beginning I had my apprehensions too. I seriously wondered if I had become so interested in Joseph as a man that I was foolishly shutting out all of the things that people were saying about him. However, I did not entertain these thoughts very long. My feelings for Joseph were quite deep and serious from the very first time I became acquainted with him.

I had been a school teacher. One in that position is generally a pretty good judge of character.

Even though Joseph was terribly reserved and kept to himself a lot, I found that my admiration for him was growing so deeply that I just had to learn more about this thing that was bringing him so much hurt so that in some way I could help him with his burden.

I remember thinking that Josiah Stoal hired a group of men and was spending a lot of money to find a mine that he had seen in a dream, yet people didn't think he was odd. They didn't persecute him!

As you might imagine, Joseph and I were doing more than just looking and smiling at each other. We were spending more and more time together. It was terribly upsetting to my parents because they had developed an open hatred toward him and were insisting that he leave our tavern. Joseph did persuade Mr. Stoal to abandon the mining project and then he went back to his folks' place in Palmyra.

Though we were separated by many miles we still kept in touch with each other by correspondence and through some of our friends. I talked my folks into letting me go and spend a short visit with the Stoals who were good friends of my parents. What I did not tell them was that Joseph would be visiting with the Knights who were friends of the Smiths' and just happened to live near the Stoals.

It was exciting to see Joseph again. We had such a good time together that we decided that we could use the same excuse to meet more often . . . and this we did.

It was during one of those meetings that we decided to get married. We knew that there was no point in consulting with my parents to obtain their permission. We realized that they would never give their blessings to our marriage. Now this would have been a mean thing to do had we not been of age, but Joseph was twenty-one years old and I would be twenty-three on my next birthday. We were married in the home of Squire Tarbill, a Justice of the Peace in South Bainbridge, New York on January 18, 1827.

Joseph and I went directly from South Bainbridge to Manchester where his parents were living. I wept a good deal on that trip. I knew that my folks would be deeply hurt and disappointed at what I had done, yet in my heart I never questioned that my prayers had been answered; that Joseph was truly the man that God had intended for me.

Joseph was so solemn as we rode along. He understood. He had already faced so much persecution and lost the love of friends and neighbors because of what he knew was right. Yes, Joseph had a perfect empathy for what I was going through. His understanding glances or soft caresses gave me all of the assurance I needed. I prayed so hard that my family would come to understand. There had been a lot of love in our home. It is quite natural when there are many children in a family that you become very much attached to each other. You see, there were Jesse, David, Alva, Phebe and Elizabeth (who was named after my mother). Isaac came next, and he had my father's given name. I came after Isaac and was followed by Tryal and finally Reuben.

Leaving my loved ones, knowing that they would not approve of what I had done, pained me deeply. Surely, I thought, they could not cast me out long. When they had thought this thing through I was sure that they would open their hearts to me again.

My parents were deeply religious and had brought us up in the Methodist faith. In fact, my mother's brother, Nathaniel Lewis, was one of the most popular preachers for miles around in our area. I honestly believed that a family with such a religious foundation would be the first to see the good in Joseph . . . but they would have absolutely nothing to do with him. Not one of my brothers or sisters ever joined the church. In fact, it wasn't until years later that Elizabeth, who had married Lorenzo D. Wasson, was friendly enough to invite us to visit with them. They were living in Dixon, Illinois at the time. You will hear more about that later.

As I was saying, we left South Bainbridge and went directly to live with Joseph's parents in Manchester. They were expecting us and had a nice room all prepared. Mother Smith said that Joseph had come home one day, (after one of our secret meetings), and very formally said, "I have concluded to get married, and if you have no objections to my uniting myself in marriage with Miss Emma Hale, she would be my choice." Mother Smith assured me that they not only approved but were delighted. It was then that they had invited Joseph to bring me to their home until we could find some other place to live.

I wrote to my family telling them about our marriage and that Joseph and I were living with his folks. I hoped that they would send me some of my clothing and personal things. You will remember that I had gone to visit with Joseph but didn't have any intention of marrying him at that time. However, during that visit he had "importuned me with such avidity!" Under those conditions I had little more with me than the clothing I was wearing. I had a good cow at home too and asked father to please save her for me.

In time I received a reply from my father and mother telling me that they had sent my personal things with a freight carrier destined for Palmyra and that my other possessions would be well cared for until such time as I wanted to come and claim them. Their love and friendliness toward me was beyond my belief. I couldn't detect any of the bitterness that I expected.

There are so many things that I could tell you about our stay with Joseph's parents. They all were so nice to us, but you can't imagine how downright mean our neighbors and the people in the surrounding area were. Joseph was a good worker and tried hard to please everyone, but they just wouldn't leave us alone. The only happiness we had was when we were alone or with the Smiths. You know it's strange there were other people in the area who were making claims regarding visions and dreams . . . they weren't persecuted! No one seemed to get excited about them or what they were saying. It convinced me more and more that the devil was fighting Joseph with everything he had to keep the truths Joseph had received from the people.

Many times Joseph had related to me the experience he had had in the grove of trees out in the field. He said that he was seized upon by some power which entirely overcame him. It seemed to bind his tongue and a thick darkness gathered around him. He felt doomed to a sudden destruction. I remember that he said that this came about not by an imaginary being, but by an actual being from the unseen world. I too was beginning to feel the power of this "being from the unseen world."

Joseph commences the work

Well, I said that we had many exciting experiences. Let me tell you about the night that Joseph and I went to the hill to get the plates. We had just been married for eight months and three days. Joseph borrowed a little carriage and a horse from Mr. Knight and we went directly to the hill. It was the 22nd day of September and the night air was chilly. Joseph left me sitting in the buggy at the bottom of the hill. I was sure that he thought that he would be right back, but he was gone for what seemed many hours. The longer he was on the hill the more my mind conjured up awful things that must have happened. I well know the power of the adversary and didn't know but what he was making one more grand attempt to stop the work Joseph had been commanded to do.

I finally saw him coming through the trees off the hill! It was nearly daylight. He had a rather heavy object wrapped in his cloak so I knew that he had finally received the "gold plates". This had been the fourth time that Joseph had gone to the hill in as many years. Each time he had received instructions from the Angel Moroni and this last time had been no exception. Joseph told me that the first time he had seen the plates he was so astonished by their antiquity and apparent great worth that thoughts of taking them to become rich and help his parents with their debts had passed through his mind. Moroni, knowing Joseph's thoughts, had then introduced him to the devil and a whole host of his servants who were standing near the place where they were.

We didn't take the plates home with us after we had received them. Joseph stopped the buggy, got out and hid them in a hollow birch log in the woods. Soon after he had thus disposed of them we were accosted by ruffians who announced that they had come to take the plates from Joseph!

It seemed that from the very moment Joseph brought the plates home to commence his work of translation that all of the powers of hell were directed toward us. People were so agitated! They were sure that Joseph did not have the gold plates, yet were spending all of their energies to take them away from us. To be perfectly honest, the ministers who had spent so much time quarreling among themselves were uniting, and with members of their congregations, coming in mob force against us.

Joseph's brother Alvin had died while they were building the home we were living in. He was twenty-five years old at the time and sorely missed by his family. It is truly hard to believe, but someone started the rumor that Alvin's remains had been dug up from his grave and had been horribly dismembered and otherwise desecrated. This caused no end of suffering to the family. Mother Smith was particularly grieved by it all. To settle the matter, Joseph's father took his boys, Joseph and Hyrum, and dug up the grave. They were relieved to find the body untouched. I tell you this experience so that you can get a little idea of how inhuman people were at that time.

I had corresponded with my parents in Harmony quite regularly. They seemed perfectly resigned to our marriage and never made any unkind remarks against Joseph and the work that he was doing. There was never any pressure put on me to come home, but instead, we were given the assurance that should we decide to come, the door latch would always be open and we would have a place to stay. Their complete change of heart was difficult for me to understand but we were both thankful for it.

With so much persecution against us in the vicinity of Manchester and Palmyra, Joseph decided to go to Harmony to further the work of translation. Perhaps it would be safer and we would find less disturbance there he thought. After all, we had received several invitations and that one hundred and fifty miles would put a lot of distance between us and our enemies. Joseph took it upon himself to write the letter asking if we might come. He carefully explained that he would be happy to work hard for what we received from them since we did not expect gratuities. However, they would have to accept the fact that he had to continue his work translating the gold plates. In miracle time, we not only had a favorable reply, but my brother Alva was knocking on our door. He had brought a team and wagon and was prepared to move us to Harmony!

There were other miracles too. I told you of the cruel and inhuman treatment we received, but it is only right that I tell you that there were a few who were real champions for our cause . . . those who really believed what Joseph was saying and doing. Martin Harris was one of these. Mr. Harris was twenty-two years older than Joseph. He was a rather wealthy well known farmer in the Palmyra area. He came to our door, told us that he had heard all of the stories and knew of the ill feelings toward us in the community, but believed that we were doing God's work. When he realized that we were leaving the area he handed Joseph $50.00! We wondered how we could settle our obligations and get enough supplies together to make the trip. Yes, our prayers were being answered.

Harmony, our first home

Joseph had put the "gold plates" and the Urim and Thummim or "Interpreters" in the bottom of a barrel of beans to transport them to Harmony. Again he had been inspired, for as we were traveling along the road out of Palmyra a group of men attacked us and went through all of our belongings to find the sacred record. All they found in the barrel were beans. I am sure that when Alva saw for himself how these men treated us that he had quite a change of heart. Alva, though he never joined the Church, did many fine things after that to help champion our cause.

I was so delighted to see how nice my parents were to us when we arrived. We stayed right in the house with them for a while. Father made arrangements with Joseph to buy some thirteen acres of cleared land and an old pelt house that Dad had used to store and cure his deer and other wild animal hides until they were sold or made into useful articles. It took a few days to remove the hides and dipping vats filled with brine. The floors and walls were scrubbed and aired, but it seemed the odors never would leave. Borrowed furniture was carried into the cleaned rooms and the small cabin became our very first real home.

Joseph worked long and hard hours. He had to work for my father to pay for the land and cabin and then use every spare minute studying the writing on the plates. I tried to help him all I could, but I was expecting our first baby and was terribly sick a lot of the time. I felt so sorry for my Joseph. Many times I heard his anxious pleas to our Heavenly Father for strength to do this very important assignment. My parents were still good to us, but when my father got behind in his work he became very impatient with Joseph. Incidentally, we wondered why we had been received so kindly when my parents had been so hostile toward Joseph in the beginning. The answer became quite clear. We

The Golden Plates — ancient records containing the everlasting Gospel

realized that father and mother felt that if they could have me near them again, they and my Uncle Nathaniel, could convince me that it was wrong to stay with Joseph. It was plain to see that they had no respect for Joseph or his special heavenly assignment. They only tolerated him because of me.

When everything seemed almost impossible, a knock came at our door. Martin Harris had come all the way from Palmyra to see us. The same feeling that had prompted him to give us the fifty dollars to help with the move had now caused him to come to Harmony to see if there was something more that he could do. He said that he had felt impressed that we needed help. Well, help he did! It was crowded and inconvenient to make room for him to stay with us, but somehow we managed. Martin never once commented negatively about our humble circumstances though I felt some embarrassment knowing what a fine home he had. I was prepared to do or accept anything to lighten Joseph's load. It was good to see his spirits improve as the two of them worked together. What a blessing to feel the strain that we had been living under almost vanish. Now I could pay more attention to preparing for the coming of our baby.

Martin would scribe as Joseph translated. This went on for a time and then Martin would have to return to Palmyra to take care of matters there. While he was gone Joseph spent more time working for father and I would scribe for him in the evenings as he worked with the plates. Several times Martin made this trip between Palmyra and Harmony. Everything seemed to be going along so well until Martin announced that he could not come back again unless he could show his wife the work that we were doing.

Joseph was crushed. He needed Martin so badly. Again I saw him plead with the Lord fervently, but he didn't seem to act like himself. He seemed so confused. I got the feeling that he just wasn't getting through to the Lord; that the Lord did not understand. Finally he gave Martin strict instruction regarding the manuscript and told him that he could take the 116 pages they had finished. I was glad to see the thing settled and Martin leave because I was about ready to deliver our baby and Joseph would have to spend most of his time with me and his work with my father anyway. After the baby came he could return with the manuscript and they would begin where they had left off.

Soon after Martin left for his home in Palmyra our little boy arrived. He was such a beautiful child. We named him Alva after my brother who had done so much to help us get to Harmony . . . but he only lived for about three hours. Joseph carried my heart out of the door with him as he took that lifeless body out for burial. I could not see him buried because the delivery had left me right at death's door. For two weeks my dear Joseph didn't get one hour of undisturbed sleep. He waited on me hand and foot. A more gentle loving man never lived.

Joseph's father and mother came to visit us soon after we lost little Alva. Since we didn't have room for them in our house they stayed in the tavern with my family. We enjoyed a wonderful visit, and I was the more pleased to see how well my parents treated them. I am sure that when the Smiths went home they felt very good about our situation here.

Joseph and I had pretty well accepted the death of our baby and though I was still having problems with my health we were anxious to get on with the work of translating. Martin had made many excuses for not returning with the manuscript, but we had to learn the truth. Joseph went to Palmyra to see what the problem was and learned that Martin had carried the manuscript all over town, laid it down on his dresser in the bedroom and never saw it again.

Joseph was a whipped man! The Angel Moroni came and took the Urim and Thummim plus the ancient record away from him. Joseph hadn't meant any harm in letting Martin take the manuscript. As a matter of fact, he was so anxious to do the work the way he had outlined it in his mind that he had failed to rely on the Lord properly. Twice the Lord had told him not to let Martin take the manuscript, and still Joseph pled! He felt that the Lord just didn't understand how important Martin was to the project as a scribe and couldn't see, at the time, why it would hurt to let him take the manuscript.

I guess the Lord wanted to teach Joseph a lesson because the third time he asked the same question the Lord told him to go ahead and let Martin take the 116 pages. Now, of course, he could understand that the Lord could get those records translated even without him and that when the Lord said no once, that it should have been enough.

The morning of the resurrection could not possibly be any more wonderful than the day when Joseph announced that the precious plates and the Urim and Thummim had been returned to him. The Lord had forgiven him of his folly and he could resume the work! Work he did! I thought he would destroy himself by it. He still had to keep my father happy, help me in the home because I had not fully recovered and resume the work of translating. I helped on the latter when I felt like it and even Alva worked as scribe for a little while.

If we show our willingness to serve Him, the Lord certainly blesses us. Just when we began to wonder how we could ever find enough time to get the translating done there was a knock at our door. This time it was a fine man by the name of Oliver Cowdery. Oliver had been teaching school in the Palmyra area. He had stayed with Joseph's parents as part payment for teaching several of the children. Of course, while he was there he had heard all about Joseph and his experiences and even though he had also heard the negative things that were said in the community he was compelled by the spirit to come on his own to Harmony to see if there was anything he could do to be of help.

Joseph and Oliver were a perfect team! My, how they worked and the spirit was always so sweet and strong between them. However, all of their hard work could not ward off the persecution that was mounting against us in Harmony. It got so terrible that even my parents caught some of the spirit of it. Oliver wrote to a friend of his by the name of David Whitmer in Fayette, New York. He told him about our work with the Book of Mormon, the problems we were having, and asked him if there was any possibility of our coming there to live until the work of translation was completed.

Within a few days we had a favorable reply . . . we were all invited to stay with him and his family. Though we had never met, we knew by the Holy Spirit that the invitation was sincere. Oliver had become well acquainted with the Whitmers when he taught school in that area. In fact, Oliver had had David's sister, Elizabeth Ann, in his class when she was just fourteen years old and I think he was very much impressed with her. At any rate, Oliver married Elizabeth Ann when she was seventeen and he was twenty-six years old. So you see, it was easy for him to suggest that we ask the Whitmers if we could come and stay with them.

As we prepared to leave Harmony to go to Fayette I became quite ill. I really hadn't fully recovered since Alva's birth. With all my heart I wanted to accompany Joseph, but we decided that it would be best for me to remain with my parents so that Joseph wouldn't have to worry about me and thus be able to concentrate on the work. It was agreed that in a short time he would either come for me or send someone to get me. Mother was extremely pleased with our decision, and father was only too anxious to see Joseph leave.

The work went well in Fayette and in a few weeks Joseph came for me. When the day of our final departure arrived, there were tears in the eyes of my loved ones. My uncle, who, as you will recall, had the reputation of being a powerful preacher in Harmony was disappointed because he had been unable to win me back into the Methodist fold. As I got ready to climb on the wagon and ride away with Joseph, my father's final words to Joseph, and he said them in a flood of tears were, "You have stolen my daughter and married her. I had rather have followed her to her grave."

As I looked back to my weeping parents, the house and yards, our first home and acres that were so familiar to me, I little realize that this would be the last time I would see them.

Do you wonder if I loved my husband?

You are probably well acquainted with all that was accomplished in Fayette. The translation was completed, the Witnesses were able to see the record, and had such a marvelous experience; the Church was organized, and I was baptized into it. With all these wonderful things happening I should not have complained, but you will never know how hard it was to have my husband as the center of attention and myself . . . nearly forgotten in the little room that the Whitmers had provided for us. It was hard to live as a husband and wife in a room that was not ours and living among strangers while all of this was going on. But Joseph was happy and excited and that was all the reward I needed.

Joseph asked me if I could "make some cloth and cut some garments with which to clothe the first missionaries called by the Church." He wanted to be sure that our missionaries looked like ministers of the Gospel instead of back-woods farmers.

I have often spoken of the persecution we received, but it is only right that I tell you that there were many who were honestly curious about the work also. These folks came from great distances at times, and wanted Joseph to explain things about the "golden record" and the work of the restoration of the Gospel.

As Joseph found the sincere, he would gather them together in various homes and have cottage meetings. There were very large crowds at times. Joseph would bear such a sweet humble testimony along with the simple story of his experiences. It seemed that angels were present at these occasions because after many meetings there were generally several who would ask to be baptized. They wanted to give their all to the work of the restoration.

Joseph explained to the people that the church would soon be organized. Then they could be baptized for the remission of their sins and for membership in the Church. He promised them also that they would receive the Gift of the Holy Ghost and that by that Spirit they would understand many more precious things of God. He also told them that once they "set their hands on the plow" they would be expected to carry the message to their neighbors and be instrumental in building up the Church in these latter days.

The Lord had said that I too should be involved in teaching the Gospel, so I can certainly say that it was a wonderful experience to attend many of the meetings, sit by the side of my husband and leave my testimony with the people.

The Church was only four months old when Joseph received a revelation from the Lord addressed directly to me! The Lord let me know that "my sins had been forgiven" and would you believe? He said "thou art an Elect Lady!"

The revelation went on to tell me that I was to be patient (I knew that I needed that counsel), and I was to comfort my husband in his afflictions. It was my responsibility to be with Joseph whenever possible, expound the scriptures if called upon, act as a scribe for Joseph when Oliver had other assignments and, being blessed with the Holy Ghost, I was to write and learn much.

As if that weren't enough, I was specifically assigned to "make a selection of sacred hymns" to be used by the Church. The Lord said, "For my soul delighteth in the song of the heart; yea, the song of the righteous is a prayer to the Lord." My, what an assignment! But I set about to do it. My formal training had been limited, but I did enjoy singing and many said that they enjoyed my soprano voice . . . at least I do recognize a good hymn when I hear one, and we did need songs that would tell the story of the restoration.

After the Church was organized it grew like a prairie fire. Of course I was delighted, but this only meant that I saw less and less of Joseph. He was traveling all over New York visiting the various branches with several of the brethren and I was alone, in a borrowed room. If the Lord would at least have let me have our little Alva. What a comfort he would have been.

On to Ohio

One day Joseph came home and said that we were going to move all the way to Ohio. The Church had taken a strong hold there and he was inspired to tell all of the saints to sell their properties and gather in the vicinity of Kirtland. On that trip we were together long enough for me to tell him that if the Lord was willing he would become a father and perhaps the sorrow left by little Alva would be somewhat healed.

With so many hundreds of people joining the Church, it seemed that we were always in the midst of strangers. However there were those special people who became our close friends and were anxious to assist us so that the ministry would not be neglected. Friends with homes and hearts to match made us welcome wherever we went.

When we arrived in Kirtland Joseph seemed to know exactly where to go. I heard him walk up to a man by the name of Newel K. Whitney and say something like, "You prayed me here, how can I help you?" It turned out that these folks had been praying to know about the true Church.

Joseph and I were made welcome in the Whitney home for several months, living in a furnished apartment upstairs above the store. Still no home of our own . . . but the Whitneys were so kind and thoughtful.

It was while we were living there on the last day of April 1831 that I had my twins, a little boy and girl and they were so frail and sickly, Joseph named and blessed them almost immediately, the girl — Louisa, and the boy — Thaddeus. They lived for approximately three hours, both dying at about the same time. You could never know how keen our disappointment was and how deep our sorrow!

On the same day that our little Louisa and Thadeus were born Brother and Sister John Murdock over in Orange, a neighboring hamlet, had twins also, a boy and a girl. Soon after they were born Sister Murdock died of the childbirth. Brother Murdock was beside himself. I am sure that he had petitioned the Lord long and hard, and then nine days after the children were born he brought them over to our house. That sweet brother stood there in tears begging us to adopt the motherless babies and enjoy them as our own. Joseph and I gladly accepted this generous offer and adopted the little infants. We named the boy, Joseph Smith

Murdock and the little girl, Julia.

For the first time in our married life we were enjoying the kind of heaven that comes with having babies. Now when Joseph was away visiting the various branches of the Church I could shower all of my love on these precious infants, trying to give them the love that their mother would have given them.

When the children were a few months old, we accepted an invitation from the John Johnsons over in Hiram, Ohio, to come and live with them. People were so kind to us. I felt as though we had been such a burden to the Whitneys, though they never complained a moment. In fact, it seems that the more problems we had the more love we received from them and the saints. You cannot believe all of the nice things that they would bring to us to make us comfortable.

We did move to Hiram which was only some thirty-five miles away. There were fewer people living there, and the Johnsons gave us several rooms to live in. Joseph had such wonderful experiences in that home. It was here that he heard the voice of the Lord again, and received so much priceless information regarding the degrees of glory and life after death. He certainly gave me a lot of comfort to know that the three little children I had lost were being cared for by our Heavenly Father.

But you know . . . the more beauty and truth Joseph received, the harder the devil fought. Oh, how it hurts to tell you of this experience. The twins were just eleven months old. They had both had a severe case of measles. Julia had practically recovered, but little Joseph was still very sick. Joseph had insisted that he sleep with him so that I could get a little more rest as I had been up with the children for several nights. This was March 24, 1832.

During the cold night some vicious mobbers broke into the house. At least four men dragged Joseph from his bed where he was sleeping with Little Joseph, beat him severely and then dragged him into the field where they poured hot tar on him and rolled his body in feathers. One of those animals clawed Joseph's bare back with his finger nails until he bled. He mockingly was yelling something about falling on him like the Holy Ghost. I was nearly out of my mind. I had run out of the house begging, pleading, and then pounding on the backs of those fiends. Because of this terrible excitement I forgot for a few minutes about our sick little Joseph in the house. The covers had been torn off from him leaving him exposed to the cold. He soon developed a severe cough and died a few days later. I will always believe that he became the first martyr to the Church in this dispensation.

We moved back to Kirtland soon after this, always sharing the homes of friends who were willing to assist. Whenever Joseph left on missionary assignments that would keep him away for a few months he would make certain that our friends would be near for help and comfort.

In the summer of 1832 Joseph received a special revelation on missionary work. He was always anxious to set the example for his brethren and never asked them to do anything that he would not do himself. I was expecting another baby and was in poor health. It was so important for him to be here under these circumstances, but he decided to go. He just knew that he could organize his work so that he could be back by early autumn when the baby was due.

Little Julia was eighteen months old and required a lot of attention. Before he left, Joseph arranged for Julia and me to stay in Hyrum's home where he felt we would get the best of care.

It was hard for me, but it was difficult for Joseph, too. I still have the letter he wrote to me from New York City just three weeks before the baby was to be born. I could tell that it was mostly his body in New York . . . his heart was with us.

Joseph had said that he would be home for the birth of the baby, but he missed it by just a few minutes. When he got to Kirtland he had run to Hyrum's home, not knowing that I had returned to our old apartment over the Whitney store. As he rushed up the stairs Jospeh heard the crying of a baby, his own son, who had been born a few minutes before.

You will never know how humbled we were to hear the healthy cry that came from our little new-born son. We were blessed at last with our own flesh and blood son. We named him Joseph Smith III after his father and grandfather.

Joseph was gone from home more and more. We still didn't have our own home and Joseph continued to leave Julia, little Joseph and me with friends when he was gone for extended periods of time.

Three and a half years passed before we had another baby . . . a boy. He was born on June 20, 1836. We decided to name him Frederick, after Dr. Frederick G. Williams, who was Joseph's counselor and dedicated, devoted friend. Little Frederick, like his brother, was the picture of health and Julia had grown into a very sweet little girl.

The Kirtland, Ohio Temple – the first temple erected in this dispensation

Just a month earlier we had received a surprise visit from Joseph's grandmother, Mary Duty Smith. This sweet little old lady was 93 years old at the time and was as alert and spry as anyone could be. She had traveled all the way from Stockholm, New York to Kirtland which was well over 300 miles. While we were enjoying our visit with her she took suddenly ill, and in spite of special blessings given to her by Joseph and his father she passed away. It was May 27, 1837 that we buried her here in Kirtland. She had lived a long eventful life and had realized her last wish, to be able to see these members of her family again.

It seemed that we did have everything in the world to live for. Oh, I guess I did envy the women who had their own homes and their husbands around them, but when I realized the importance of Joseph's special calling, and that I also had these wonderful children, life was beginning to have real meaning. Though Joseph was gone frequently he never failed to let us know how special we were to him, and how much he needed us.

As I have said before, whenever we began to feel a measure of success or personal happiness, Satan would show us what he could do. It was hard to see and hear the slander that was leveled against my Joseph! It was more difficult to realize that some who had formerly held positions in the Church had become apostates and were then some of Joseph's most hated enemies.

From Kirtland to Missouri

Some of our most severe difficulties resulted with the failure of the Kirtland Anti-Banking Safety Society. Joseph had warned the brethren for a long time to stop their wild land speculations. People were trading in real estate in Kirtland and thinking about nothing but getting rich. Then, of course, it happened! So many of them lost all that they had when the Kirtland Safety Society failed. Joseph had warned the people, had even withdrawn from the Society, asking others to follow his example but they would not listen. The temple had just been completed and dedicated. Joseph and Oliver had the privilege of conversing with the Savior, Moses, Elias and Elijah; receiving such important keys from them! Within such a short time it was almost impossible to hold a priesthood meeting in the temple without it breaking up into a riot. There was only one thing to do. Joseph came and told us that we would all have to leave Kirtland and join the Saints in Missouri.

Independence in Jackson County had been dedicated as the Center Stake of Zion. Many of the saints had migrated there and were building up the area. I knew though that they were having their troubles too. Jealousy, the slave question and just the same old devil inspired persecution had followed them there. I wondered how we could find peace and safety there, but we had to go. Joseph could not even travel with us. There were many who were threatening to take his life. Oh, how it grieved my Joseph to have enemies like that and see me and the little ones suffer so. There was nothing to do but trust that friends would help me and the children while he took a different route to Missouri where hopefully we would meet again. You know, now as I think back, it would have been so easy for me to take the children to Harmony and live a near normal life, but, very honestly, that thought never entered my mind. We were committed to Joseph's heavenly assignment to restore the gospel to the earth!

It was a bitter experience, and when we got to Missouri it was not one whit better. All of the reports I had heard about the sufferings among the saints were certainly true. The Missourians had a general hatred toward us and treated their animals better than the Mormons. Joseph sheltered us with some members in Far West while he spent endless hours working to establish Zion as he had been commanded.

It was the Spring of 1838 there in Far West. I was expecting another baby, and would you believe it — Joseph actually came home one day before the baby was born! This was another plump healthy little boy! He looked so much like my side of the family that we decided to name him Alexander Hale Smith. Right after we named him Joseph said that the name surely fit, because we were right in the middle of another "halestorm"! Feelings were running so strong against the Mormons that the governor issued an order to drive every Mormon from the state or "exterminate them."

The saints at Haun's Mill had been deprived of their fire-arms and then without warning 240 horsemen under the leadership of Colonels Jennings and Comstock rushed upon the village and started to shoot at the thirty defenseless families living there. Volley after volley descended on the men, women, and children.

The only ones to escape were those who hid among the trees and dense underbrush. The attackers jumped from their horses and stripped what clothing and valuables they wanted from the dead and dying and then weeks later were boasting about their foul deeds.

While this was happening at Haun's Mill those of us settled at Far West were completely besieged by mobs. Threats were heard from all corners. Joseph was in extreme danger. He never seemed to worry as much for himself, however, as he did for his family and the safety of the saints. Oh, those were trying times! Little Alexander was not a year old, and Julia, little Joseph, and Frederick also needed constant attention. In addition, Joseph's father and mother were with us . . . and his father was so very sick.

Joseph's incarceration

It is a long story, but suffice it to say, Joseph was betrayed into the hands of the enemy by the apostate "Judas" Hinkle. Joseph, Sidney, Lyman Wight, Parley Pratt and George Robinson were handcuffed, chained and staked out in the open all night long while a bitter cold rain, mixed with snow, fell on them.

I learned that Joseph was to be shot to death at 9 o'clock the next morning, over on the public square. Oh! Man's inhumanity to man! What had Joseph done to deserve this awful fate?

The next morning I heard rifle shots . . . I thought my dear husband was dead!

General Doniphan had received the order to execute Joseph, but unbeknown to me he had replied to General Lucas that he would not carry out such an order since it was cold blooded murder. He further warned General Lucas that if he thought to execute these men he would hold him responsible before an earthly tribunal if it was the last thing he did!

Joseph was alive, that was most important. It was the second day of November when Joseph and the others were marched home to say goodbye to their families before taken off to prison. Joseph asked his captors if he could have a private moment or two with his family but this was not allowed. The children and I wept and clung to their father until the swords of the guards separated us, and my Joseph was taken away.

The first real storms of the winter were setting in. Few of the saints had enough to eat or warm clothing to cover their bodies. It was share and share alike in order to stay alive. We suffered and thought that conditions could never be worse until we learned that we were no longer able to stay in Missouri . . . and had no where to go. As I previously mentioned, Governor Boggs had issued his infamous "extermination order." This had the same effect as declaring an open season on all Mormons just as you would treat wild game. The burnings, plunder, rape, and murder that followed that vicious governmental order!

Brigham Young, John Taylor and Heber Kimball took the lead of the Church in Joseph's absence. They had been able to communicate with Joseph from time to time while he was held prisoner, and therefore were carrying out his wishes as best they could.

Word had reached us that Joseph had been taken first to Independence, and then on to the Richmond jail. On the way to Independence Joseph told the brethren that the Lord had assured him that their lives had been given them and whatever they might suffer in captivity, not one of their lives would be taken. This was a great comfort to me, to Joseph's father and mother, and other members of the immediate family.

Brigham had written to the governors of several states asking for their permission to find asylum with them. There had been poor response. We did learn, however, that the people of Western Illinois understood our plight. They organized welfare committees and gathered food, clothing and money for us as well as opportunities for some of the brethren to find employment with them. One fine old man in Quincy even offered to give Joseph and me a house to live in.

There is no point in lamenting about it now, but it is true that many families traded their homes and improved farms for as little as a single yoke of oxen. The Missourians knew that we were compelled to leave, so we couldn't expect any different treatment.

Joseph had spent endless hours with Sidney Rigdon revising the Bible giving us an Inspired Translation. Various people had helped to carry and protect the Bible that he used as a text and the manuscript. As we left Missouri it fell my lot to safeguard these things. I sewed two pockets in the underside of my skirt, one on each side, and put the five pound Bible in one and the equally heavy manuscript in the other. In my arms I carried two of the children and attempted to shield the others as well as Father and

The Liberty jail where Joseph was imprisoned for many months

Mother Smith from the bitter cold as we left Missouri to find another home. The Saints were scattered all along the Mississippi seeking shelter as best they could as we migrated toward Quincy.

On the fourth day of April I received a letter from Joseph. He spoke briefly of being "under the grimace of the guards night and day, and within the walls, grates, and screeching iron doors of a lonesome, dark, dirty prison . . . ". Joseph expressed his great love for me and the children. He seemed particularly anxious that the little ones not forget him. He said, "Tell them Father loves them with a perfect love and is doing all he can to get away from the mob to come to them." He went on, "Father says they must be good children and mind their mother." Joseph feared that the ungodly examples that the children had seen would have too much affect on them.

I learned that while Joseph and the other brethren were in the Richmond jail they were being slandered by guards who were boasting of defiling by force "the wives, daughters, and virgins, and of shooting or dashing out the brains of men, women and children." Brother Parley Pratt said that all of a sudden Joseph rose to his feet and though he was in chains he commanded, "Silence ye fiends of the infernal pit!" and then in the name of Jesus Christ commanded them to be still . . . saying that he would not "hear another minute of such talk or they or he would die that instant!" The guards quailed in a corner at his words and trembled in his presence. The Lord had spoken through my divinely inspired husband.

Our sufferings were great, but the brethren in prison suffered also. They spent those cold winter months sleeping chained to a cobblestone floor with no heat except a little fire built occasionally on the floor . . . but with no place for the smoke to escape. Their bed was a pile of straw and the food so putrid that only extreme hunger forced them to eat it. It was even rumored that they had been served "mormon beef", the flesh of some unfortunate human being!

Joseph received several revelations while he was in prison. He must have been very near the breaking point when he wrote, "O God, where art thou. And where is the pavilion that covereth thy hiding place? How long shall thy hand be stayed, and thine eye, yea, thy pure eye, behold from the eternal heavens the wrongs of thy people and of thy servants, and thine ear be penetrated with their cries?"

The Lord answered those please by reminding him, "The Son

of Man hath descended below them all. Art thou greater than he? Therefore, hold thy way, and the priesthood shall remain with thee . . . fear not what man can do, for God shall be with you."

After we had found a temporary shelter in the vicinity of Quincy the brethren insisted that I go back to Missouri and visit my dear Joseph in prison. The Saints gathered some clothes, blankets, and food to share with the prisoners and since we had been assured that the Missourians would allow this visit I took the older children with me. I knew that Joseph, should I really get to see him, would thus be especially pleased.

All went well on this trip and I was able to embrace Joseph again. The children were frightened at the first sight of their father and the others, but in a little while were on his lap and about his neck. I knew then that God was mindful of us.

It was hard to leave, but Joseph assured me that the Lord had promised him that no one would lose his life and he felt that it would not be much longer until we would all be reunited.

When the children and I returned to the saints, we were filled with encouragement. The people in Illinois were so kind, and were doing everything they could to make us welcome. It also appeared that the brethren had found an opportunity to buy some large tracts of land on up the river with promissory notes.

Joseph and I had prayed so hard that we might be blessed with children to raise to adulthood . . . and then when we had our little ones amid all that persecution, hunger, and cold, I wondered if we had done the right thing in asking for them. However, now that the suffering had abated I realized that these children, my husband and the Gospel were more precious to me than life itself.

Joseph eventually escaped from his captors. In fact, the guards were so disgusted with the treatment given the prisoners that they traded some of the things the prisoners had for one of their horses, and while these guards drank their liquor, Joseph rode off to join us in Illinois.

Are there words adequate to express oneself when you see our beloved husband, haggard, weary, and tired standing there looking at you . . . when you had nearly given up hope of ever seeing him free again?

He was here, he was alive, but he also belonged to the saints. God just had to sustain him in all that he was doing. No mortal man could muster all of the strength that he had. His very presence seemed to still the fears of the hundreds of homeless saints much as the Savior stilled the fears of His disciples when he calmed the waves of the sea.

Building the "City Beautiful"

There was not time to be idle. We soon settled on the land that was purchased with the notes. The area was known as Commerce, but appeared to be quite worthless. There were only ten or twelve log cabins to be seen for miles around and much of the land was a bog. Joseph, however, could see how the bog could be drained and used as land for building part of the city. Not just an ordinary Western town, but a model city with a beautiful white temple that would be seen for miles in either direction as one approached the city on the river.

It was May of 1839 when the Church members started to drain the swamp, build houses and shops and clear the land for farming. Joseph knew that though this was not the Zion spoken of by the Lord, it would be a city modeled after an inspired plan. There was so much sickness to begin with in Commerce. We had had so little proper food, clothing and bedding. There was little resistance to disease, and the very air around the swamps seemed to give people a kind of a swamp fever.

The saints had insisted that Joseph and I and the children live in an old log house by the river. We had Joseph's parents live with us, and though it was crowded, we fared very well compared to those who were living in tents and wagons. Then too, there were many living in the open without any protection. Once, when the sickness was so severe, Joseph had us move into a tent out in the yard so that the sick and dying could have decent shelter until other provisions could be arranged. It was soon after this that Joseph changed the name of our city from Commerce to Nauvoo . . . Nauvoo means "city beautiful". In a very short time there were approximately two thousand hand hewed log houses, three hundred beautiful brick homes, and between two and three hundred frame houses in our city. Much of the lumber for the houses had to be hauled all the way from Wisconsin. In addition to the houses there were many brick shops, stores and even cultural centers throughout the city . . . not to mention the beautiful temple taking form on the hill.

We had a continual stream of people coming to our city . . converts, dignitaries, as well as others who were interested in the Gospel or just plain curious. Since housing was at a premium the Brethren decided to build a "Mansion House." It would have twenty two rooms . . . large enough so that our family could live

Nauvoo, Illionois — "The City Beautiful" on the banks of the Mississippi

there and also have plenty of room for overnight guests. As soon as this Mansion was completed a "Nauvoo House" was also to be built. This building would have been one of the largest lodges along the Mississippi, but, as you know, it was never finished as it was intended.

Joseph was so busy with all of these projects and spiritual matters that he completely forgot to record the birth of our son, Don Carlos, in his journal. Our baby was born June 13, 1840. We named him in honor of Joseph's younger brother who idolized him very much. Don Carlos, like his brothers Joseph, Frederick, and Alexander, was the picture of health. Julia was also doing very well, developing into a lovely, beautiful young lady.

I had some trouble finding time to finish the assignment given to me by the Lord to collect appropriate hymns. I gathered a little here and a little there but it was some time before the hymnal was published. Eventually it was printed in Nauvoo by the E. Robinson press. They had no way of printing the musical notes, but since the words were generally sung to familiar tunes we managed very well. The title page made me very happy·

A collection of sacred hymns for the Church of Jesus Christ of Latter-Day Saints, selected by Emma Smith.

"In order to sing with the Spirit, and with the understanding, it is necessary that the Church of Jesus Christ of Latter-Day Saints should have a collection of SACRED HYMNS adapted to their faith and belief in the gospel, and, as far as can be holding forth the promises made to the fathers who died in the precious faith of a glorious resurrection, and a thousand years' reign on the earth with the Son of Man in his glory. Notwithstanding the Church, as it were, is still in its infancy, yet, as the song of the righteous is a prayer unto God, it is certainly hoped that the following collection, selected with an eye single to his glory, may answer every purpose, until more are composed, or until we are blessed with a copious variety of the songs of Zion."

Frankly, I felt that I had done very well. I had gathered a total of three hundred and four hymns.

Family sickness and sorrow

With everything going so well, we were hardly prepared for the blow that fell so suddenly. On the seventh day of August 1841, Joseph's brother, Don Carlos, passed away. He died in his twenty-sixth year leaving a lovely wife and little children. Joseph was so fond of this devoted brother, and was heartbroken with his passing. He spent many hours writing several pages of history about him, paying tribute as only Joseph could.

Scarcely had he finished his writing, however, when our little Don Carlos took suddenly ill and passed away, just eight days after his namesake. Little Don Carlos was 14 months old when he died. Our first three children had lived but a few moments; their deaths had been difficult to bear, but little Don Carlos had been with us for over a year, making his loss almost unbearable! He had been walking for a few months, and had learned to speak many words which had been such a delight to us. Yes, I know what grief is.

The day after the baby's death, Joseph was to conduct a conference of the Church in Nauvoo, but he could not find the strength to go. Never had I seen him grieve so.

Early the next afternoon, Joseph did decide to sweep the sorrow from his heart by activity among the saints whom he loved so dearly. Wiping his eyes, he went to the conference. He arrived after the meeting had started, and as he walked through the crowds towards the rostrum that was in the grove on the hill, perhaps a thousand silent prayers were breathed in his behalf. A few moments later he was at his customary place at the pulpit where he spoke at length. It was as if he taught his listeners by his shining example that no personal sorrow or heartache should hinder the progress of the glorious work in which we were all engaged.

I guess I have to be honest. I received nearly all of my strength from Joseph and my precious children. Joseph had us, but he also had the saints and the constant demand on his time. These seemed to help him overcome personal sorrow much faster than I was able. However, I could see a change come over him too. The death of his brother and our little Don Carlos took its toll with him. He seemed to be so serious much of the time. It wasn't that he did not have faith in the resurrection and an understanding of death. Not long ago, when speaking at Brother King Follette's memorial service, Joseph explained the beautiful principle that tells us that "God was once a man, as man is today, and that as God is, man may become." He had had the privilege of seeing his older brother, Alvin, after Alvin had died, and knew that he would inherit the Celestial Kingdom. There was all of this, but it seemed that Joseph was trying to find more happiness for us here on earth, and at the same time he was leaving the feeling with us that his family and many of the saints would be unable to find it.

I mentioned that Joseph's father was very sick as we came out of Missouri. We nearly lost him then, but pleaded with the Lord through special priesthood blessings for his life. As things settled down a little here in Nauvoo he continued his activities as best he could, but was never really well. Don Carlos had died on the 7th of August, our little Don Carlos on the 15th and now it seemed that Joseph's father would never be able to regain his health. He had been ordained a Patriarch some time ago, and like Jacob of old, he called all of his family to his bedside and gave each a special father's blessing. On September 14, 1841, when he was 69 years, two months and two days old, Father Smith was laid to rest behind the old homestead next to Don Carlos.

I was still numb over the loss of our little son, but as I looked into Mother Lucy's eyes I realized that perhaps she knew more about suffering and loss than I did. I silently vowed with my Heavenly Father that I would do all in my power to take care of this sweet mother, not out of duty, but because our sufferings, over the years, had welded our hearts together.

On March 17, a beautiful Spring day in 1842, Joseph called all of the prominent sisters in Nauvoo together. He said that we had been so assembled to organize, under the direction of the Lord, the women's Relief Society of the Church. The objective of the Society was: "the relief of all the poor, and destitute, the widow and the orphan, and for the exercise of all benevolent purposes."

Joseph then caught me completely by surprise as I heard him say "I now propose that Emma Smith, our Lady Elect, be sustained by your uplifted hand as the president of this Society."

The vote was unanimous. Joseph then went on to explain the seriousness of the assignment given to our organization. He said, "This is a charitable society, and according to your natures, it is natural for females to have feelings of charity and benevolence. You are now placed in a situation in which you can act according to these sympathies which God has placed in your bosoms."

With this challenge, and with words of extreme soberness

Joseph continued, "If you live up to these principles, how great and glorious will be your reward in the Celestial Kingdom! If you live up to your privileges, the angels cannot be restrained from being your associates."

The Lord must have given me this assignment so that I could lose myself more in the service of others and not have so much time to think of my own problems. The society was certainly needed.

Joseph and I were expected to be leaders in the happy festivities that took place around the Christmas season, and we usually did have many friends and saints in our log home. Joseph was very much in favor of sponsoring these happy occasions, but during the Christmas season of 1842 we took no part in public celebrations. You see, I was soon to give birth to another baby, our tenth, counting our adopted children, and Joseph was at my side almost constantly. It was as though he knew that we would have another heartache and he wanted to do everything he could to give me strength.

I got so sick that I couldn't do a thing to prepare for Christmas or even do more than just wish Joseph a happy birthday, his 37th. He spent Christmas day at home filled with anxiety. Julia was eleven years old at the time, old enough to help care for the smaller children. Little Joseph was ten. What a Christmas it could have been for the family. Of course, our friends did all they could for us, but there was a terrible, ominous, feeling in our home.

The day after Christmas Joseph had to attend court in Nauvoo. He was ordered by that court to go to Springfield, the state's capitol to stand trial on the same charges and would have to leave the next day in order to make the assigned appointment.

While he was making preparations to go I got very sick and gave birth to another son. The little boy was still-born. What can I say?

Joseph was obligated to leave me and the sorrowing children while friends buried the still-born child. Those who went with Joseph told me later that they had never seen Joseph as solemn as he was on that trip. They said that there was no question but what Joseph wept inwardly during the whole time. His body was in the carriage and in the courtroom, but his mind was with his grieving family back in the log home in Nauvoo.

The Missourian menace

Earlier that year ex-Governor Boggs was shot and seriously wounded by a would-be assassin. Mr. Boggs tried to blame this whole incident onto Joseph saying that he had dispatched Porter Rockwell to do the shooting. Boggs was successful in getting Governor Carlin of Illinois to issue a writ of arrest for Joseph and Porter. Joseph said all along that if Porter had done the shooting he would not have missed and botched the whole matter. Anyway, because of that terrible incident Joseph was in and out of the courts and had to spend so many days and nights away from us. He could well remember the months of imprisonment in Missouri and did not want to repeat those experiences. Governor Reynolds of Missouri declared the writ issued by Governor Carlin illegal but there was a thirteen hundred dollar reward offered for the apprehension of Joseph and Porter and they were not going to take any chances of being caught.

You know, when Joseph returned from that trip to Springfield (at the time we had the still-born child), he found me very depressed and physically uncomfortable. That sweet noble man acted as though he didn't have a problem in the world except making me comfortable and happy. Without a word to me he went over to Sister McIntire's house. She had just had identical twin girls and Joseph was determined to get one of those little girls for me to nurse, care for, and love. It no doubt took a lot of persuasion but he succeeded! Sister McIntire let Joseph bring little Mary to me for several hours a day for quite a period of time. At the previously agreed upon hour, Joseph would personally return Mary to her mother with the promise that he would return promptly the next day to pick her up again.

Joseph was happy because I was happy again. He loved little babies and children as much as I did. It was one of earth's most beautiful pictures to see him take little Mary, wrapped in her silk quilt, or one of our own children on his knee and, while trotting them up and down, either singing to them or making funny noises to get them to smile or laugh.

One morning Sister McIntire handed Sarah to Joseph instead of Mary when he came for the baby. Even the mother had a difficult time telling which was Mary or Sarah, but Joseph immediately said, "This isn't my little Mary." He became so attached to that little girl. After Mary was no longer brought over to our house Joseph would frequently stop by the McIntires' to play with and talk to her.

Mary took suddenly ill and passed away. Joseph and I grieved for her as though she was one of our own. I remember that Joseph held her cold little body in his arms and said, over and over again, "Mary, oh my dear little Mary!"

Perhaps few men were as tender-hearted and affectionate as my Joseph. His love for us knew no bounds. I am absolutely convinced that some of the saddest hours of his life were the ones that took him from his home and family.

I don't quite know how to explain it, but it seems that from the time that we lost our last son and Joseph's trip to Springfield, that the very jaws of hell opened to devour us. The mobbings started all over again. People who were living on the outskirts of our beautiful city were having their homes and crops burned. We had a large number of men under arms, but how do you fight an enemy that you cannot see. You could bring the people into the city for greater protection, but the biggest fires burning against us were started by the apostates and disgruntled within the Church. . . much the same as it had been during the days of Kirtland and Missouri.

Celestial Marriage

Persecution started anew over the doctrine of celestial marriage that Joseph had introduced to the brethren. When he gave it to them he also tried to give it to me. He didn't have the courage to tell me himself, he sent Hyrum and the bishop over to tell me about it. I will admit that I reacted violently. I was so shocked that I burned the revelation up! I could not make myself believe it! However, knowing my Joseph, I saw him deeper in depression than I had ever seen him, and as you know, we had been through a lot together. He told me that he would rather die than impose such a practice on me, but it was the will of the Lord and he had gone against this counsel for as long as he dared.

With the whole matter out in the open Joseph proceeded to explain it to me. It seems that many years ago Joseph had been studying the scriptures and could not understand why David and Solomon, not to mention Abraham and Jacob, had more than one wife. He went to the Lord, like he had always done when there was something that he did not understand, and learned that these men did not commit adultery because their plural wives had been given them by the Lord through his prophets. Further, Joseph learned (and this was such a severe blow to him) that he was to introduce this practice first among the Brethren, and then to the faithful Saints to build up a righteous seed.

We were suffering so much persecution when Joseph received the revelation that he chose to ignore the instruction he had received. He was reminded from time to time and finally received what he called the "Drawn Sword Revelation." An angel with a sword drawn approached him and asked him if he was going to follow the commandment or if the Lord was to look for another man to take his place!

I was hurt, both by the doctrine and to see my Joseph suffer so. He went on to tell me many things about this doctrine that I admit I could not understand at the time. He told me that he had already had women sealed to him and that the official beginning of this practice was when Bishop Joseph B. Noble sealed his wife's sister, Louise Beman, to him. It seems that Joseph gave Bishop Noble the key to this power and told him how to go about performing the ceremony. I was shocked and hurt as I listened, but in all honesty I can see why Joseph had kept it from me for so long. (He had done this in April 1841.) After all that time we had

The Nauvoo Temple – built with great sacrifice of the Saints

been through, no man would willingly impose such a doctrine on his wife. Joseph had also received a revelation commanding me to accept those sisters who had been given to him before I had knowledge of plural marriage. No wonder, that as a last resort, Joseph sent Hyrum and the Bishop to present the revelation to me. I knew that I would never have a second place in Joseph's heart, so I not only forgave him for what he had done, but consented to the practice and brought some of the eligible sisters over to the house and stood at their side while they were sealed to my beloved husband.

Some of the leading brethren of the Church had been commanded to follow Joseph's example but this was not, as yet, a principle or practice for the whole church. That time would come.

It was on or about the 12th of August of 1843 when the revelation was openly presented to the Nauvoo high council. Joseph told me that it was accepted by a nine to three vote.

I had long ago learned that it was not an easy matter to do all that God commanded, but I had also seen the rewards that came with obedience so I tried hard to accept this principle having faith that all would work out well in the end.

One day I heard Joseph say, "The Savior had his Judas, and now I know that I have mine." I didn't know exactly what he meant, but it left me so very sad; Joseph was so lonely!

Joseph had given the sacred priesthood endowment that he had received by revelation to a number of the brethren, and told me that the sisters were also to be privileged to receive this ordinance. He carefully instructed me as to its purpose, the procedure in giving it and the blessings that came from it. While I certainly did not hold any priesthood I functioned under the direction of the priesthood and thus became the first "female ordinance worker in this dispensation." Elizabeth Ann Whitney became the second. The anointings releating to this endowment were given in our home and Bathsheba W. Smith, the wife of Joseph's cousin, George A., was one of the first sisters to receive her endowments. Of course, we officiated with the women while Joseph, and later others, officiated with the men.

As I came to understand the endowment I also received glimpses of the eternal world that made earthly things more understandable.

The Mansion House, a splendid home

The Mansion House had been pretty well completed and Joseph left the children with some of the sisters while I was given the privilege and responsibility of taking some other friends and traveling down river to St. Louis to pick up furnishings and carpets for the 22 room hotel mansion. Joseph did not go with us for fear of being recognized in Missouri, but even without him it was one of the nicest trips I can remember. Joseph said that we should buy fine things for the house because in a way it represented the Church, and those who came to visit with the saints should be properly entertained.

We moved into the beautiful home soon after the boat load of furnishings arrived. I never dreamed that we would be able to live in such a beautiful place. It was a mansion where many came and were entertained, not only with food and lodging, but for business and many wonderful social events were also held there. And we had a home! A place where the children found so much happiness. We lived rather royally, I like to think.

All of this, however, could not fend off the persecution that was springing up all around us; the apostates, the Missourians, the disgruntled, the very devil himself. Joseph was almost constantly in hiding from his enemies. He was not concerned for his life, but the Lord had told him to run the church, and he knew from previous imprisonments just how hard it was to run the church from a jail.

It was June, 1843. We were having such a difficult time being together as a family, Joseph decided that we would quietly leave Nauvoo and go up state to Lee County and visit with my sister, Elizabeth, and her husband, Benjamin Wasson. They had invited us and since Dixon was some distance from Nauvoo, we thought we might find some much needed rest and togetherness there.

The devil works overtime! We arrived in Dixon all right, but scarcely had we done so when two men, pretending to be our missionaries, were directed to where we were. They accosted Joseph right in front of the house. "These ruffians, with blasphemous oaths threatened to shoot Joseph if he so much as stirred."

Poor Joseph replied, "I am not afraid of you shooting. I am not afraid to die. I have endured so much oppression, I am wary of life, kill me if you please . . . but if you have a legal process to

The stately Nauvoo "Mansion House" — the final home of Joseph & Emma

serve I am at all times subject to law, and shall not offer resistance."

Threats, accompanied by horrid blasphemies were again and again repeated by these so called gentlemen of the law, who, hurrying him off to the carriage they had waiting, without permitting him to say farewell to his family, and without serving any legal process upon him, attempted thus to kidnap him.

These men took Joseph into Dixon and locked him up in McKennie's Tavern. Joseph shouted out of the window to some men that happened by, "I am falsely imprisoned here, and I want a lawyer."

A lawyer came and the Missouri ruffians banged the door in his face. Another came and received the same treatment. A crowd immediately gathered, told the sheriff that Mr. Smith should have justice done him, and if his captors persisted in refusing it, they would find a summary way of dealing with them; they might so act in Missouri, but in Illinois a man should have his right. Writs were served, considerable traveling was done, the case was heard and Joseph was set free to return to us.

I should tell you that Stephen Markham and William Clayton had heard in Nauvoo that Joseph's life was in danger, so they rode 212 miles in 64 hours to warn us. Of course, they arrived after Joseph had been taken. However, they went on into town and, after seeing what had happened, they quickly secured a warrant for the arrest of Mr. Reynolds and Mr. Wilson.

My what a circus! Sheriff Campbell of Lee County arrested these two and Joseph was supposed to be under their arrest. But that is still not the end of this experience. You see, William Clayton rode with all of his might back to Nauvoo to tell Hyrum what was going on. They both feared that other attempts would be made to carry Joseph off into Missouri so Hyrum called on the Nauvoo Legion. One hundred seventy-five men marched from Nauvoo determined to prevent any force from taking Joseph out of Illinois.

When Joseph saw the men from the Legion he said, "Well, I guess I won't go to Missouri this time. There are my boys." As I said, courts could not find Joseph guilty of anything, but that did not stop the persecution or other attempts on Joseph's life.

On another occasion there were a number of men in town determined to arrest Joseph. His friends decided to take him to another hiding place in the dead of the night. As he saw none of the enemy about he asked the brethren to take him home for just a few minutes. Joseph rushed in, held me in his arms for a few minutes, and then led me to the children's bedrooms where we knelt and I heard him breathe a prayer for them. Then he kissed them and me and was soon in the carriage and on his way to that new place or refuge.

Joseph had become a fugitive in the beautiful city that he had worked so hard to build. He was hunted by gangs of the most wicked fiends imaginable. The only time he could come into the house was when we were absolutely sure that none of the enemy was about. Our home was watched day and night because the children and I were there and those seeking my husband knew of his devotion to us. So that we could see each other once in a while, he would send messages to me telling me where he was and I would meet him at these hiding places for a brief visit. One night he might be hiding in Brother Granger's cabin on the outskirts of the city; another time in the basement of Brother Egbert's house or in the attic of another friend's home.

Joseph came home once, thinking that none of the enemy was about. We were eating dinner when a knock came at the door. Brother Boynton was with us, so he went to the door, and when he realized that our visitors were Missourians, he spoke loudly so we could hear and detained them long enough for Joseph to get out the back door and hide among the tall corn stalks in the garden. (From there he made it over to Bishop Whitney's home where he stayed for a time). Our unwelcomed guests apologized for not having a search warrant, but asked if they could go through the house looking for Joseph, they had been so sure that they had seen him enter. I laughed and told them to come right in and search all they wanted. I guess it was a grave disappointment to them when they mounted their horses and rode away, doubtless assuring each other that the wanted man must be far from home.

As often as possible Joseph would go up on the hill and mingle with the workers at the temple. He was very anxious for the temple to be completed so that they could do work of the endowments there. As soon as one portion of the sacred temple was complete those rooms were dedicated and that part of the endowment ceremony and instruction was carried out.

Across the street from the temple lot our most bitter persecuters opened a print shop. They published one issue of a newspaper called the "Expositor." It vilified the Saints, and scandalized the wives and daughters till the city council declared it a nuisance and had the press destroyed. As I see it now, this was the beginning of the end for us.

Joseph seemed to know that the sands of time had run out. He begged Hyrum to take his family and go to Cincinnati. Hyrum wouldn't leave, so then Joseph asked others to please talk him into leaving. Joseph kept saying that he wanted Hyrum to stay alive so that he could avenge his blood. Hyrum held priesthood keys equal to Joseph, and Joseph wanted that power protected. But Hyrum was not the kind of man to leave his brother when things were not going well. All he would ever say was, "Joseph, I just can't leave you . . . come what will . . . you can't make me go!"

One of the brethren told me that he heard Joseph tell Hyrum that if he was ever taken again he would be massacred, or he was not a Prophet of God, and if Hyrum insisted on staying he would be massacred with him.

Joseph had been talking for some time of exploring the West as a possible place for the saints to settle. He wanted to take us so far away from established communities that no one would want to follow. With everything so upsetting, Joseph was determined to leave the country and spend his time looking for a new home while, perhaps, things settled down here. He had organized the Western Exploration Company some time ago to gain all of the information they could regarding the region known as the Rocky Mountains. He felt he might as well take Porter Rockwell and some of the other brethren and see what the West was like . . . where hopefully we could get away from all of our enemies.

Joseph was out on the island in hiding while Porter and the others were busily getting essential supplies together. As this was going on a posse from Carthage came into Nauvoo to take Joseph . . . to stand another trial. When they learned that he was away they said they would remain in Nauvoo until Joseph returned if they had to wait forever.

A number of the saints had learned of Joseph's intentions and some began to call him a coward saying that he was running to save his own life with no regard for theirs. I thought of the many times the Lord had seen us through difficult situations so I sent him a note asking him to please come back; that he was being called a coward and it was just more than I could take.

When Joseph received my message he counseled with Hyrum and Porter. The three decided to come back, even though Joseph had warned Hyrum that he would be killed. When I saw him he was very solemn. All he could say was, "If my life is of no value to my friends, it is of none to myself."

The Martyrdom

I remember how Joseph's frequent references to death had unnerved me greatly, yet I didn't have the same feelings he had. We had gone through similar crisis before. This too would eventually pass away.

Joseph was restless all night long. He spent most of that troubled night pacing the floor. Several times he went into the children's bedrooms and stood gazing at them. He held me in his arms as we tried to comfort each other without much success.

Early the next morning a number of the brethren, including faithful Hyrum, came to the house to ride to Carthage with Joseph. Joseph didn't appear to be quite so solemn, but I see now that he was trying to make the parting less sorrowful for the children and me. He held us tightly, kissed each of us, and then rode away. He had not gone far, however, when he returned with the excuse that our dog, Major, must be put in the house so as not to follow them. He seemed happy for the excuse to tell us all goodbye again. It was during this final farewell that Joseph said, "Now Emma, I promised not to talk about it again, but if something should happen to me, and if the baby you are carrying is another son, please do me a favor and name him David Hyrum. I have always like that name."

My eyes were glazed with tears as Joseph rode out of sight. A few moments later Major jumped out of an upstairs window and ran down the road to join his master!

I understand that Joseph got part way to Carthage when he was met by a company of the Carthage Greys under Captain Dunn. They had been ordered by the Governor to go to Nauvoo and take all of the state owned arms away from the members of the Nauvoo Legion. Captain Dunn was afraid that he would run into serious trouble in Nauvoo so he induced Joseph to return with him. Joseph was in the city for a few hours, but he didn't come back home.

Three days later a friend rode up to the house in the middle of the night and told me that Joseph and Hyrum had been shot to death and that Brother Taylor was seriously wounded. My world came to an end! I knew that he was telling the truth, but after all Joseph and I had been through I could not make myself believe it. Mary, Hyrum's wife, soon came over with her children as did Mother Smith. They too were completely stunned!

Carthage jail, site of the martyrdom of Joseph & Hyrum

It was the 28th of June, Dr. Willard Richards, who had been in the jail with Joseph and the others, and Samuel, Joseph and Hyrum's younger brother, brought the bodies of our loved ones home. There were others too, but I don't remember who they were. All I know is that the Saints literally lined the side of the road for miles waiting for the wagons with the bodies to come. Their moans, sobs and cries rose like an eerie tempest. I couldn't do anything but try to comfort my precious children and myself by doing all I could for them and Mother Smith.

When they arrived, Joseph was in one wagon box and Hyrum in another. They had been covered with buffalo robes and green twigs and boughs to protect them from the heat of the summer sun. As the procession arrived at the Mansion House there were hundreds of people milling about. I got to the wagon just as the branches and robes were removed. There lay my Joseph! His face was contorted as though in extreme pain. His eyes were partly open, and his skin ashen white. There were pieces of straw and chaff from the crude mattress in his touseled hair and on his blood stained clothes.

I don't know if it was the intense heat of the day, or the forbidden glance at my dear Joseph's body, but I fainted away. Mary had pled with me not to go out, but how could I restrain myself. The next thing I knew I was in my room with some of the sisters bending anxiously over me, trying to bring comfort. Mary, Mother Lucy, and our children were all weeping bitterly. It was not just a bad, bad dream. Joseph and Hyrum were dead!

After what seemed endless hours, the door opened and we were told that we could see our husbands, the children's fathers and dear Mother Smith's sons. Two of the sisters walked at my side as I entered the room. The bodies were on day beds by the west windows of the room. I started toward Joseph and then fainted again. When I awoke I could hear Mary sobbing, "Oh! Hyrum! Have they shot you my dear Hyrum?" She had drawn him close to her bosom and was kissing his pale lips and face, stroking his hair with her hand. The children had surrounded her and their dead father. Their sobs and groans were more than I could stand. I fought so hard, but fainted again.

Mary was still at her husband's bed when I entered the room the second time. I was determined to go, with my children, to my dear husband. Someone tried to assist me, but I pushed them away. I remember walking past Hyrum and his family and then feeling a strength come to me, knelt at the bedside of Joseph. His cool cheek against mine brought me strength. Strange that Joseph could bring me comfort even at this time. I remember talking to him through my sobs, asking him if he was really dead, begging him to open his eyes and hold us just once more. The children seemed to be braver than I. They were all at the bedside weeping, but I felt that they were weeping as much for me as for the loss of their father.

There were so many people in the room. I wanted very much to be alone with him and the children just once more, but he belonged to everyone. I could only stroke his gentle face, hold him close and speak to him in whispers.

In time, the crowd was asked to leave the house. They were promised that the next day would be set aside for all to come and pay their last respects.

We sat up all night long with the bodies of our husbands. Never have I known such grief. In fact, I know that this grief turned into a bitterness worse than gall.

Early the next morning the bodies of our beloved were placed in specially prepared coffins. These coffins had been covered with a black velvet, held in place by brass nails. The inside was lined with a white cambric.

At 8 a.m. the house was opened to the saints who had come to view the bodies and pay their last respects. I just could not stand to meet all of the people. They meant well, but how could they understand? Joseph and I had been married just seventeen years. I kept asking myself, "Now what have I got?" I had my children, and I was sure that I would see my husband again on the other side of the veil. But was this emptiness the reward for all of the suffering we had endured together? We never had a decent home to live in until now, and had only been able to enjoy this for less than a year. We had our God, too, but I began to wonder, seriously wonder. Why, why, why did he let Joseph get killed in such a cruel manner? He wouldn't even get to see his unborn child. All of these thoughts went through my mind time and time again as the children and I secluded ourselves in a hot upstairs bedroom waiting for the endless lines of people to go home and leave us alone. Thousands passed through the Mansion that day. The scene was indescribable. At 5:00 p.m. a request was made to clear the Mansion so that we could take our farewell look at the remains.

This time when I saw Joseph his skin had turned an ugly dark color and the stench of the dead was so bad that vinegar was boiled on the stove to cover the odor! I wondered if I could live through that horrible experience.

The bodies with the coffins were taken into a little bedroom in the northeast corner of the Mansion and there concealed behind locked doors. Sand bags to simulate the weight of the bodies were placed in the outer boxes that had been intended to cover the coffins in the grace and then the boxes nailed up. A mock funeral took place and the boxes were put into a hearse and driven to the grave yard by William Huntington and there deposited in their graves with the usual ceremonies. It was thought that some Missourians would be sacreligious enough to dig up the grave and sever Joseph's head so that they could collect the ransom that had been placed on it.

About midnight, some of the men who had been sworn to secrecy took the coffins with the bodies out and buried them in the basement of the unfinished Nauvoo House. It rained torrents that night, yet I wonder if it equaled the flood of tears I shed.

It seemed that I had scarcely buried Joseph when Brigham Young came to the house to get what he called Church records, and I had a feeling that he was trying to tell me what to do, acting as though he was the head of the Church. I suppose that he was trying to be kind, but he was not the man to stand in Joseph's place. If anything, our little Joseph should head the Church, and I could take care of things until he was old enough to assume the responsibility. Who had been clsoer to Joseph than I?

Nothing seemed real any more except that Joseph was dead. My children were fatherless, and my unborn would never see his father. Maybe it was all my fault, I sent for Joseph to return when he wanted to go West. I told him that the saints were calling him a coward.

I had given up my home, parents, everyone of my brothers and sisters, everything to follow Joseph and the gospel. Now all of the visions of what had been and what was supposed to be were gone. Lost. Seventeen years I lived with Joseph. I might just as well have been buried with him.

Life in Nauvoo without Joseph

There were a number of men who claimed a right to run the church other than Brigham. James J. Strang, Granville Hedrick, Sidney Rigdon, Lyman Wight, and David Whitmer. When Joseph's only living brother, William returned home from the East he also tried to get the people to let him run the church. He was an apostle, and Joseph's only living brother. Would you believe, the new organization promptly excommunicated him from the church . . . accusing him of all sorts of foul deeds. This was too much! The Smiths had given everything, and then they were nothing. Didn't the Lord, through a beautiful revelation, call me "Lady Elect?"

It is true that Mary, Hyrum's wife, and Mother Lucy did not see things as I did. I could not understand how Mother Lucy took it all. As if it was not enough for her to lose her husband in Nauvoo, and then Don Carlos, Joseph and Hyrum, and then Samuel on the 30th of July, only a month after Joseph and Hyrum were killed. As a matter of fact, Samuel was hurt when he went to Carthage to help his brother and never did get better. And then the brethren took the church away from William! He was bitter, as you can imagine, and he did everything he could to keep me from going West with the others. I was not about to do it anyway, but Mother Lucy had spoken of it. William soon straightened her out. Why should she leave all of her loved ones here in Nauvoo to follow old "Bogus Brigham?"

Lucy did not have the bitter feelings I did. She still associated with the saints like Mary did, but I guess my light had gone completely out. I decided that I did not want anything more to do with the church. I turned away from all of our former friends too. I just wanted to be left alone! At first I tried to hide my feelings about Brigham but as he persisted in his 'bossy' attitude I came out in open rebellion against him. He was just not the man to stand in Joseph's place! To be honest, I was not prepared to see any man in that position. They said that Joseph's authority . . . that is, the authority he received from heaven, now rested with the Quorum of the Twelve. However, it seemed to me that Brigham did all of the talking. It was just too much for me. All of the brethren who supported Joseph when he was alive were now rallying behind Brigham with the same dedication and enthusiasm they had given to Joseph.

They kept after me to do my work as president of the Relief Society. I asked them to release me, and though they didn't, I still refused to go. How could I direct the women who looked at me as though I had gone out of my mind? I was also invited to go to the temple to do some sealings and endowment work. I made up my mind that I would never set foot in that place either . . . even though I had administered the endowment to many women in the past. Lucy, Mary and the others attended, but they could do as they wished, I was through! All of their attempts to fellowship me seemed to drive me further away. I didn't want my mind to dwell on the past, and I could not live in the present.

It is all very hard to explain; those who were eager to show their faith and support for Brigham and the other leaders truly got on any nerves! I found myself literally hating these people and lashing out in every way I could to hurt them. For example, I saw people praising Mary for her bravery and dedication. They looked up to her with so much adoration. Mary and I had been good friends, we had much in common . . . she had not done anything to hurt me, but I found that it made me feel good to hurt her. I don't know why I did it! I have so much to repent of.

One day I went over to Mary's house, I can't remember what for, but I happened to see Hyrum's gold ring that I had admired in the past. I asked if I could see it, and then refused to give it back to her. She cried bitterly as I walked off with it. I also took an oil painting of Hyrum's and refused to give that back either. Why did I do those things? It was so opposite to my nature before Joseph was killed.

Brigham directed the people to prepare to leave Nauvoo and go to some unknown place in the West. That was just fine. I felt that if they got out of here, then maybe I could live in peace. I found that I wanted to rid my mind of everything that reminded me of the past.

I got worse as the time approached for the birth of my baby. Oh, how I remembered the look on Joseph's face as he spoke of his fears of not being able to return to Carthage, and that he wished for me to name the baby David Hyrum.

November 18, 1844. How proud Joseph would have been to see his son, David Hyrum! When this beautiful little boy was born it seemed to me that all of the old wounds were made a little deeper. I could see his father buried in the floor of the unfinished Nauvoo House. I couldn't stand it! Mary did not agree, but I insisted that Joseph's body be moved from that place and given a decent burial

Exodus of the saints from Nauvoo, across the great Mississippi to the West

behind the old homestead. I didn't go when the grave was opened, but my little twelve year old Joseph went. When he came back from the awful experience he said that he had seen his father's features when the coffin was opened and one of the men cut a lock of hair from his father's head. My son gave me the lock of hair. I put it in a locket, in fact I am wearing it now.

When they moved Joseph's body they also moved Hyrum's at the same time. Mary acted as though she didn't care one way or another by this time, but I felt much better. It was another secret burial but at least they were not resting in the cellar of that house and were nearer to Father Smith, Don Carlos and Samuel.

When the Saints started to leave the city I had the strangest feeling come over me. I saw all that was happening around me, but felt completely isolated from it. Brigham and the council gave us everything we needed, even the assurance that they would take care of us as long as we would accept help, whether we went West with them or not. They no longer talked to me about going with them and I knew that with them gone I could live in peace. My world revolved around my children and Mother Lucy.

It was quite a different citizenry that moved into town after the saints left. I thought that I would feel better with them gone, but the hollow feeling inside of me persisted.

Joseph once wrote, "Again she is here, even in my seventh trouble . . . undaunted, firm, unwavering . . . unchangeable! my affectionate Emma."

What happened to that Emma? Oh, I needed help in my "seventh trouble."

I truly believe that the emptiness was worse than some of the severe persecution we had gone through. Then we were fighting for something! We were together . . . we felt emotion, life was real!

I decided to take my children away from Nauvoo and see if I could find myself in another place. A Mr. Van Tuyl had offered to rent the Mansion from me, so I decided that I would accept his offer. I felt that we could get along with the rent money and perhaps find something else to supplement our income. I did not have any place to store things so I rented the Mansion completely furnished; bedding, dishes, cookware . . . everything.

Joseph and I had been up to Dixon, Illinois, you will remember, to visit my sister Elizabeth and her husband. We had gone through a pretty little town by the name of Fulton that was right on the Mississippi. I decided that I wanted to go up there and live . . . and there we went. It was difficult to wrestle the children and all of our luggage, but as I thought of our new life, a fresh start, it all seemed a small enough price to pay. After all, I had gone through this kind of thing many, many times before. Then, however, we were nearly smothered with friends trying to help. Now we were alone. At least the children were older. Joseph and Julia were especially helpful and the weather was beautiful.

We were only in Fulton a shorttime when I received word that Van Tuyl had not been able to get enough boarders or people to stay in the Mansion to make it a paying business. The note I received from a neighbor informed me that Tuyl was not only leaving without giving me notice, but he was taking my dishes, bedding and furniture!

We packed up the same day the note came and took the steamer back to Nauvoo. I caught that rascal red handed! The neighbors had detained him long enough for me to get there. He left town all right, but not with my belongings.

The next few years of my life were lonely indeed. It was hard to provide for my five children, and the boys especially needed a father. We still had the farm and our garden. The church, out West, continued to send us some support. Mother Lucy came over quite often. She nearly always spoke of the past: her husband, Joseph, and others who had passed on. She talked without any bitterness and I found that I could tolerate what she said as long as I didn't reflect too long on it. If I did, a feeling of panic would come over me . . . as though something would come along to hurt me or some member of my family again.

The new citizens of Nauvoo who had moved in to take over the properties left by the followers of Brigham Young generally minded their own business. Nauvoo became a sleepy little village with far too many houses, schools and shops. Many of these soon went into decay. What a contrast!

I continued to operate the Mansion House as a place where the traveler could obtain a meal or a night's lodging or both, but I didn't have much business.

Two or three very fine men came around from time to time and wanted to keep company with me. When I felt that one was getting serious I would send him away for good. In my heart I knew that it would be right for the children to have a man around to help bring them up, but . . . as much as I loved Joseph, I did not want another man here as a living reminder of him. It would be too much like pulling a scab off an old serious wound.

Major Lewis Bidamon

Strange, isn't it? How time and circumstances put a different light on things. During the summer of 1847 Major Lewis Crum Bidamon started to drop in, not as a boarder, but he seemed to show a genuine interest in me, and I was surprised that I did not feel the panic I had before when suitors had come to see me. The Major . . . as everyone called him, had been in the state militia some years back and received his title then.

He too had been married before and rather recently buried his wife. He was such a direct opposite to what Joseph had been. I guess that was why it didn't seem to bother me when I thought of being married to him. He was tall, had dark hair and dark eyes, as contrasted to Joseph's light hair and blue eyes. He dressed well and considered himself to be quite a sport. One day as he came to see me he went out of his way to visit with some of the children who were playing on the lawn (I was watching from the window, unbeknown to him). As he proceeded toward the door he didn't notice that I had strung a clothes line between two trees . . . he looked so chagrined as he picked his hat and toupee off the ground. We all had a good laugh at the Major's expense.

I knew that Lewis frequented the bars and liked to drink with his friends. (I didn't learn until later that he was also quite a gambler and had a bad reputation in other things that were anything but desirable). His parents had been devout Methodists, but he had not absorbed much religion.

My boys seemed to like him, and he in turn showed a special interest in them. We saw more and more of each other, and it was no surprise when he proposed marriage. He suggested that we get married just before Christmas, but I put him off. You will remember that Christmas was always a big event with us because of Joseph's birthday and all; I couldn't do it then, but on the 27th of December we went over to Reverend William Hana, the Methodist minister in Nauvoo, and were married.

It had been three and one-half years since we lost Joseph. I was forty-four years old when I remarried and Lewis was two years younger.

The children seemed pleased when the Major moved into the Mansion with us. He had a small store in the city where the boys found employment. Lewis also took charge of our farm which was two and half miles east of the city. In addition to the farm we had a large garden by the Mansion where we raised our own vegetables and kept our cow, horses, pigs and chickens. The Major had been a harness maker and was quite expert with tools and leather. The boys were taught to work, but I noticed that Lewis was more of a promoter than a worker.

The tourist trade at the Mansion dropped off to almost nothing. About the only people coming to Nauvoo for lodging were Mormon missionaries stopping over on their way to their assigned fields of labor in the east or Europe. They were interested in seeing where perhaps they or their folks or other friends or church leaders had lived. They always tried to engage me in conversations, but though I often knew them or their folks, I avoided their questions. I did gather from the talk among themselves that Salt Lake City was growing rapidly . . . as was the church.

The Major wasn't much of a provider. He was more interested in 'get rich' projects without much work attached and which generally involved gambling. It didn't bother him at all to sit in the house and spit his tobacco on the side of the pot-bellied stove while the boys and I did the chores and the work around the house and yards.

I was truly crushed when I learned that Lewis had gone out and fathered a little boy by Nancy Abercrombie. It was obvious that Nancy wasn't pleased to have this baby so I told Lewis to bring him home to me. We named him Charles. He was a delightful child, and my children accepted him almost immediately as a member of the family. Their maturity was a constant amazement to me.

Lewis fell in with a man by the name of Nathan King and went out to California for a time to get in on the gold rush. I learned though that there was not much of an opening out there for an executive and the digging was too hard. He did open a small shop where he repaired mining tools and made wooden handles for picks and shovels. What money he made he soon lost with his gambling and came home with hardly a dime.

Mother Lucy passes on

When he returned, we moved out to the farm where we could take better care of it. Lucy left the house that Joseph provided for her and moved in with us. She was seventy-six years old and almost completely helpless. I really loved her, and felt a keen satisfaction in taking care of her. I guessed it helped my conscience a little and gave me a tie with the past that somehow was pleasant and good to live with. Lucy was good to me, too, and never criticized me for the way I was living. The Major liked her too, and didn't seem to mind in the least that she was living with us. In fact, he went out and got some material and in a very clever way attached wheels to her chair so that she could get around the house by herself.

Before Lucy died we had moved back to the Mansion House. She set aside one of the rooms where she put a number of things on display that had belonged to Joseph, Hyrum, and others. When the Utah missionaries and others came around Lucy would charge a few pennies for each one to see the things she had gathered. This gave her an opportunity to get a little pocket money and also have a visit with her guests. She especially loved to ask the missionaries about her former friends, the church leaders and everything in general. She was kind enough, however, to leave me out of the conversation.

Just two months before she would have been eighty years old, Lucy went to bed at her usual hour in the Mansion House and died in her sleep. When she passed away it was like another chapter of my life closing. I loved the dear old lady, the mother of my Joseph, very much, and it was never a burden to care for her. I guess I sort of felt that anything I did for Mother Lucy I was doing for Joseph.

Our children grow up

Life went on. Julia married and moved to Texas. The boys continued to run the farm. They were also branching out into businesses of their own. My young Joseph studied law, and held several offices of public trust. He was justice of the peace for a number of years, served on the board of education, had been a merchant here in town, and also ran the farm.

Joseph married a beautiful young lady by the name of Emmeline Griswold when he was twenty-four years old. They often visited with us, and it was especially interesting to hear him talk about the things he remembered about his father and what he did when he was alive. He often remarked that the happiest days of his life were when he had had the association of his father. There was always something exciting about the hustle-bustle that went on then. He would talk about the many happy hours he had spent on his father's horse, Charlie, accompanied by Major, our beautiful and intelligent dog. It was quite a different Major that he had come to know as his stepfather.

As I said before, our Major had no interest whatever in religion, even made fun of it. I found that young Joseph developed many of Major's ideas and attitudes. Our whole family "dropped out" of religion. Again, I cannot explain it. I knew that all of the things that Joseph and I had struggled for were true, but I found myself running away and even vocally denying many things that he had taught and represented. It seemed I did everything I could to keep the ghost of the past from rising up to hurt and haunt us.

George A. Smith and Erastus Snow made a special trip out here from Salt Lake to see if they could talk Joseph into joining them and moving out to Utah. I don't suppose that they offered him any particular position in the church, but they did plead with him to be "one" with them and do what he could to help build the church and his father had given his life for. Well, Joseph wouldn't have a thing to do with them and even displayed an open hatred toward them.

I mentioned before that I certainly was not the only person who could accept Brigham Young, and that several men tried to rally folks to follow them in their cause. Some succeeded more than others.

William, Joseph's only living brother, worked rather hard to teach the people that the principle of "lineal descent" applied to the presidency of the Church. He spent a considerable time holding meetings in Wisconsin, Illinois and Michigan. This was around 1850 to 1853, but he was not like his brothers. He could not get the people to respond to him.

At the same time William was trying to work up a following there were other men who had much the same idea. William Marks had been stake president in Nauvoo, but Brigham had him excommunicated. President Marks joined the Strangites for a while and then later attached himself to a group headed by Mr. Charles Thompson. He was not happy there either so in 1855 he joined with John E. Page who had been an apostle under Joseph. Jason W. Briggs had also joined with Strang, later he claimed that he had had a revelation tellng him that my boy Joseph should be the head of the Church. Zenos H. Gurley had the same information revealed to him, so he got together with Brother Briggs and they invited the others to join with them in using their influence to get young Joseph to come along. I know that they came to visit Joseph at least three different times.

I heard Joseph tell these men, when they first came around that he could "tolerate discussions of politics and weather or anything but religion."

Strange, even though I had lost interest in religion, something inside was urging me to get Joseph to accept their offer. It felt good in my mind's eye to see my son standing at the head of the church. I guess it was a way of fighting back at those who were trying to run Joseph's church. Maybe, I thought I could destroy some of their smugness.

I don't suppose that Emmeline, Joseph's wife, took much of this talk seriously bit I will admit that I began to try to show Joseph that he could re-establish his father's church and not have any persecution if he did away with those things which had brought the saints, his father, and me so much unhappiness. It was no problem to convince him and others that plural marriage, temple endowments, work for the dead and the plurality of Gods . . . plus many other objectional principles were all Brigham's ideas. Joseph had instituted these things, but anyone could see that was why we had had so much trouble with our neighbors. If Brigham Young was given the blame for these things it might cause him to suffer and lose his power, and we could then bring Joseph into a better light here. Brigham probably blinded Joseph anyway and caused him to accept those things.

It was no easy matter to get Joseph to see the wisdom of heading this church that had grown out of the various splinter groups. As I said before, Joseph had no interest in religion. However, as the months passed by he seemed to give a little. Zenos Gurley and Mr. Briggs were kind and patient with him. A steady pressure from them and me seemed to melt his stubborn heart. He finally reached the point where he would say that he would accept the proffered position when he felt like the spirit had directed him.

It was more than three years later, and sixteen years after the death of his father, when Joseph finally caught the spirit of this new movement. On April 4, 1860, I went with him to the village of Amboy, in Lee County, Illinois, where I saw my son Joseph ordained as president of the Reorganized Church of Jesus Christ of Latter-day Saints. He was ordained by Zenos H. Gurley, William Marks, Samuel Powers and William W. Blair. Outside, it was a cold miserable rainy day, but I was warm!

I had my name put on the membership rolls of this new Reorganized Church, but I did not take too active a part in the church. I was pleased, however, to see the matter settled and my sons active.

The bitterness in me just would not let me have peace. Lewis never was interested in religion as I have said, and I found that as the children got older he took less and less interest in us too. He was content to spend most of his time with his cronies drinking and gambling. He was two years younger than I, and seemed very anxious to preserve his youth.

More and more of the Utah missionaries came to Nauvoo to see the city and of course, they continued to come to the Mansion House for meals and lodging. Our house was badly run down and in need of repair, and it bothered me considerably to have them come and see Lewis spitting his tobacco juice on the side of the stove in the living room. He was usually under the influence of liquor and loud with profane oaths and dirty stories. He would sit there like that while I tended to all the work.

I could see that the Utah visitors looked at me in surprise and then pity. Often they would try to engage me in conversations regarding their people. There were times when I would like to have visited with them but some kind of a hurt, way deep inside of me, kept me from any association with them. I continued to find that I was happiest when I could be all alone, alone with my memories.

It seemed that my boys all grew up over night. All four of them were very active in the Re-organized movement.

Some years later Alexander and David went as missionaries to the Salt Lake Valley. They had an interview with Brigham Young, but reported that they had a very cool reception, I would not have expected anything different. They asked Brigham if they could use the tabernacle to preach in but were turned down flat! The boys had a number of cousins out there as you know, but they were hardly civil with them.

All of this did not completely discourage Alexander and David, however, they managed to hold some meetings in homes and a few halls and did succeed in teaching and converting some of the Brighamites.

I stayed pretty close to Nauvoo all the rest of my life. I did go up state in Illinois once when I learned that my brothers and sisters: David, Alva, Elizabeth and Tryal had moved there, but they did not act too excited to see me so I did not stay long. I learned that Tryal and her daughter were killed in a tornado just a few days after I left.

Memories

Julia was the first in the family to get married. She and her husband, Elisha Dixon, took over the Mansion for a little while after they were married. I moved back into the old homestead. Elisha had been an entertainer by profession, worked with magic and called himself the "gypsy king." There was not enough doing in Nauvoo to keep him occupied so they moved on and I took the Mansion over again. Shortly thereafter Elisha was killed in an explosion on a river steamer. He left Julia a widow while she was still in her early twenties.

Julia came home to Nauvoo and lived with me again. Some time later she met and married John Middleton. He took her to St. Louis and I learned that he was down-right mean to her. He drank heavily and never let her talk of home. He was "strongly opposed to Mormonism" and to keep peace with him Julia joined the Catholic church. She could not abide Middleton and his drunken rages so she left him and moved back in with me here in Nauvoo. Julia never had any children and therefore showered all of her love on me and my grandchildren.

About five years after Frederick was married he became ill and all of our care could not save him. He died leaving his widow and sweet little daughter Alice Fredericka. Fredrick was only twenty-six years old when he passed away.

With our adopted children, Julia and Joseph, Joseph and I had had eleven children. Now only Julia, Joseph III, Alexander, and David are left. What a reunion the others must be having with their father and grandparents.

To be honest, I really don't have much left to live for. The children are all so busy. I see them and the grandchildren from time to time, but it seems that they have their interests and problems now. I always tried to have cookies on hand for the little ones. Even the children in the neighborhood call me the "cookie lady" and find it convenient to stop by often. But this is not enough to make me feel like I am needed, or of much worth. I must have been forty-one years old when I married Lewis. We never had any children together, so when my children left we just sort of tolerated each other. If I should die soon Lewis will be just fine. He knows how to work his friends to get just what he wants.

It has been nearly thirty-five years since we were married. The seventeen years that Joseph and I were together seem like a dream, even though we went through so very much together.

We are living in the Riverside Mansion now. The Major had it constructed some time ago from much of the material intended for the Nauvoo house. Our house is actually on part of the foundation of the intended Nauvoo House and, as a matter of fact, over the first resting place of Joseph and Hyrum . . . they were buried inside of the original walls of the house.

Time has a way of moving on and I feel that my time has come. I haven't been feeling well, and my family has been staying pretty close. I suspect that they too have a feeling that I will not be with them much longer. Julia has been such a blessing to me. She is always here when I need her.

The boys have been at my bedside a number of times and we have had such pleasant visits. It seems that all they want to talk about is when their father was alive. Just today Joseph asked me so many questions and then said, "Mother, what do you really feel about the Book of Mormon?"

71

When I started to talk I could see that he was writing it all down, so I talked slowly. I told him, "My belief is that the Book of Mormon is of divine authenticity. I have not the slightest doubt of it. I am satisfied that no man could have dictated the writing of the manuscript unless he was inspired; for when your father would dictate to me hour after hour; and then when returning after meals, or after interruptions, he would at once begin where he had left off without either seeing the manuscript or having any portion of it read to him. This was a usual thing for him to do. It would have been improbable that a learned man could do this; and, for one so unlearned as he was, it was simply impossible."

Joseph seemed pleased. I had not had much to do with religion over the past years and I guess he thought I had completely lost my faith.

I suppose that I should be thinking of many things that ought to be settled before I leave mortality and meet my Maker. These things I have thrashed over and over. I believe He will understand. Strange, I too "feel so calm as a summer's morning."

It would be nice to be laid to rest by the side of Joseph. I know about where his grave is, but then I could miss the spot by quite a little, so I have asked the boys to lay me to rest under the big lilac bush behind the Homestead. You know, you can learn a lot when you close your eyes and breathe a little heavy so that they all think you are asleep. I heard the boys say that the city council told them that no one could be buried on private property any more and it looked for a time that they could not honor my last request, but then the city fathers recognized this as a special situation . . with Joseph buried there and all. I don't think that lilac bush is far from where Joseph's body is resting.

David wrote such a fitting tribute concerning his father and his final resting place. He called it "The Unknown Grave." After he wrote it he also set it to music and we sing it in our regular church meetings. I understand that the Utah Mormons sing it too.

> "There's an unknown grave, in a green lowly spot,
> And the form that it covers will ne'er be forgot.
> Where heaven trees spread and the wild locusts wave
> The fragrant white blooms o'er the unknown grave.
>   Over the unknown grave."

It goes on for a number of verses and each is so touching . . .

"The prophet whose life was destroyed by his foes,
Sleeps now where no hand may disturb his repose.
Til the trumpets of God drown the notes of the wave,
And we see him arise from that unknown grave.
Arise from that unknown grave."

Maybe someday they will find that unknown grave and at least place a suitable marker over it.

It gives me so much time to think . . . just lying here.

Brigham Young has been dead for two years. We never got along, but I will have to admit that he kept his promise. He sent Mother Lucy and me money and special gifts on many occasions. I heard that he did the same for Sophronia, Catherine and Lucy, Joseph's sisters, even though they didn't go West either and joined the church with my boys. Yes, I will have to admit that he tried to do what he could, under the circumstances, to show respect to Joseph's memory by remembering his loved ones. You certainly have to give him credit for that.

The church didn't stop growing under Brigham's direction . . . and the persecution didn't let up either. I never will forget how the last of the saints were driven out of Nauvoo. My, some were so old. The smart aleck rough necks that took over the place threw some of these old folks right in the river saying they were baptizing them in the name of Joseph Smith. They had to be fished out, near drowned, and hauled over to the other side where there was some safety for them. I guess the mobs pretty well knew how I felt and that's the reason they didn't give us any trouble.

Those Brighamites really suffered crossing the plains. They tell me that some 6,000 graves were dug along the trail between here and the Salt Lake Valley. Imagine, the government even declared war on them and sent Johnson's army out to Utah! It certainly reminds me of our Missouri days. Joseph was in the thick of it then, and I have a feeling that he would have been out there doing the same thing if he were alive today. All of his very closest friends and co-workers are there. They are growing too, in spite of the persecution . . just like it was when Joseph was alive.

We don't have any problems with our neighbors here. We never have had any serious problems . . . except against the Brighamites.

Oh, how can I judge any more than someone can judge me. I was willing to fight and struggle right along with Joseph and the rest of them when he was alive. My how it hurt to see the little ones, old people, the sick . . living worse than animals; driven from their homes in the dead of the winter! Strange, I could take all of that because I knew that we were doing it to establish God's Kingdom on the earth again. We received the strength from Him. That is where it came from! How did I get so confused? Where did I lose this tremendous spirit?

Oh! Joseph, Joseph. Please redeem me from this awful hell!

Epilog

It was April 30, 1879 . . . the twins, Louise and Thaddeus had been born on that day . . . and now Emma Hale Smith Bidamon "turned her face and gazed upward; her last words were, "Yes, Yes! I'm coming Joseph. Joseph!" She quietly breathed her earth life away, and her worn body sank to rest.

Emma died in her seventy-sixth year. Was it Joseph to whom she said, "I'm coming?" I truly believe that it was. She was given to him by the Lord as a "help meet" suitable to the assignment of the restoration. In this she did not falter. When she changed, the work was well established. It would have been wonderful had she "endured to the end," but who among us can judge her life after the death of the Prophet? Who can understand the workings of the mind when time after time it is brought near the breaking point. And then, finally, her husband is brought home to her, his face . . ashen white, clothes matted with his own dried blood, and his breath silent. He would never open his eyes again in mortality or see the son that was stirring in Emma's womb to remind her that not all was lost. It is one thing to put the pieces of a body back together when it is torn apart, but who understands this great human mind? Oh, be careful as you judge Emma, dear reader. Be compassionate!

Emma was buried beside a large lilac bush not many feet from the unmarked grave of Joseph. The Major was seventy-four years old when Emma died. He married again soon after her death and continued to live in the Mansion. Not much can be found regarding him except to say that he lived to the age of eighty-five and died on February 11, 1891.

Joseph and Emma
"Eternal Companions"

In 1928 the Reorganized Church determined to find the graves of the martyrs so that a suitable monument could be erected. Considerable time was spent interviewing some of the older residents of Nauvoo to see if they could learn where the old spring house had stood under which the Prophet and Hyrum were buried. They tested the soil in many places to find where it might have been disturbed, and after much time, effort and money the two skeletons were found. Both skeletons bore the scars of the martyrdom. The unknown grave had been found! A number of the citizens of the town of Nauvoo were invited to examine the remains.

New graves were prepared immediately behind the old Homestead. Emma's remains were also removed and placed beside those of her husband and Hyrum. A large long slab of concrete was placed over their graves with the inscription: Joseph Smith, Jr., Emma Hale Smith, Hyrum Smith.

Special Note

In her book *(Joseph Smith, The First Mormon,* Doubleday & Company, Inc., Garden City, New York, 1977) Donna Hill makes the following interesting observation:

"Apparently after he surrendered to Governor Ford at Carthage, and shortly before his martyrdom, Joseph sent a message to Emma telling her to write a blessing exactly as she would like it, and he would sign it when he returned. In that document, *which exists in her own hand,* Emma reveals her humility, piety and courage, and between the lines, her heartache, 'I desire the Spirit of God to know and understand myself, that I might be able to overcome whatever of the tradition or nature that would not tend to my exaltation in the eternal worlds. I desire a fruitful active mind, that I may be able to comprehend the designs of God, when revealed through His servants without doubting . . . I particularly desire wisdom to bring up all the children that are, or may be committed to my charge, in such a manner that they will be useful ornaments in the Kingdom of God. I desire prudence that I may not through ambition abuse my body and cause it to become prematurely old and care-worn, but that I may wear a cheerful countenance . . . and be a blessing to all who may in any wise need aught at my hands.

I desire with all my heart to honor and respect my husband as

"Final resting place"

my head, ever to live in his confidence and by acting in unison with him retain the place which God has given me by his side, and I ask my Heavenly Father that through humility, I may be enabled to overcome the curse which was pronounced upon the daughters of Eve . . . that whatever may be my lot through life I may be enabled to acknowledge the hand of God in all things.

These desires of my heart were called forth by Joseph sending me word . . . that he had not time to write as he would like, but I could write out the best blessing I could think of and he would sign the same on his return.'

Tradition has it that Emma never saw Joseph alive again."

Appendices

The question is often asked, "What became of Joseph's and Emma's children?" Also, very little is ever said about Joseph's sisters: Sophronia, Catherine and Lucy.

It is interesting to find that Joseph's parents also had eleven children even though Joseph only mentions nine when he tells his own story *(Pearl of Great Price, Joseph Smith 2).* Children who died in very early infancy apparently were not frequently mentioned since the infant mortality rate was so very high.

Using information gathered from: *The Saints Herald, Vol. 118.9:53, 1971* by Richard P. Harward and *The Family of Joseph Smith* by Cecil E. McGavin, Bookcraft, 1963, plus other minor sources, I have abbreviated their information regarding the children from both families.

Appendix A

The children of Joseph Smith Jr. and Emma Hale Smith

1. **Alva.** Born June 15, 1828 and died the same day.

2. and 3. **Louisa** and **Thaddeus.** Twins born April 30, 1831. They both died shortly after birth.

4. and 5. Joseph Smith Murdock and Julia. Twins born to Brother and Sister John Murdock. The mother died when the twins were born. Nine days later they were presented to Joseph and Emma by the father to be adopted by the Smiths.

Joseph died when eleven months old, March 31, 1832, due to severe exposure when his father was beaten, tarred and feathered. "The first martyr in this dispensation."

Julia died one year after Emma in 1880 at the age of forty-nine. She had married twice (Dixon and Middleton). Julia died childless. Cecil McGavin writes that as Julia was dying of breast cancer her full brother John R. Murdock, came to see her. John had come from Utah and was going on a full-time mission for the church. Julia was being cared for by a James Moffett and his wife who lived on a farm near Nauvoo.

John stayed around Nauvoo for a month, perhaps waiting to see if there was any chance that his sister would live. When he left he gave the Moffetts enough money for Julia's medical and burial expenses, plus some for a marker for her grave. Julia died a few days after John left and was buried in the Catholic cemetery in Nauvoo.

6. Joseph Smith III. Born November 6, 1832. He was twelve years old when his father was martyred. He married Emmeline Griswold when he was twenty-four. They had four daughters and one son. The son died in infancy. Joseph III and Emmeline moved to Plano, Illinois and Emmeline died there.

Three years later Joseph III married Bertha Madison. They had four sons and five daughters. This wife died as the result of an accident in 1896.

In 1898, Joseph III married Ada Rachel Clark. They had three sons. Therefore, Joseph III had seventeen children by his three wives. He passed away December 10, 1914 at the age of eighty-two years. He had been president of the Reorganized Church for nearly fifty-five years.

7. Fredrick Granger Williams Smith. Was born on June 20, 1836. He married Annie Marie Jones when he was twenty-one. They had one daughter in 1858, Alice Fredricka, and no sons. Fredrick lived in the Nauvoo area all of his life and was a farmer and merchant. He died in Nauvoo at the age of twenty-six on April 13, 1862.

8. **Alexander Hale Smith.** Born June 2, 1838 in Far West, Missouri. Alexander married Elizabeth Kendall when he was twenty-three years old. He lived for a time in the Nauvoo area where he was known for his athletic ability and skill as a hunter. He was very active in the Reorganized Church and traveled extensively as a missionary for the Church. He served as an apostle and as a counselor to the president of the church. During his last years he served as the Presiding Patriarch.

He was the father of four sons and five daughters. Alexander died on August 12, 1909 while visiting the old Mansion House in Nauvoo. He was seventy-one years old.

9. **Don Carlos.** Carlos, as he was most often called, was named after Joseph's brother. He was born in Nauvoo, June 13, 1840 and died suddenly August 15, 1841. His uncle had died eight days earlier, August 7, 1841.

10. **Stillborn child.** No name given. Joseph says that a day or so after Christmas in 1842 he had been in court and "on my return home, I found my wife, Emma, sick. She was delivered of a son, which did not survive its birth."

11. **David Hyrum.** David was born on November 18, 1844, five months after his father was killed.

It is said that "he was a very striking, impressive character, having the most outstanding personality in the family."

David married Clara Hartshorn at the age of twenty-six. Their only child, Elbert, was born in the Mansion House in Nauvoo.

David Hyrum was very active in the Reorganized Church serving as missionary and counselor in the First Presidency. He was an excellent poet, writer and painter.

David was very emotional and sensitive. He suffered from a nervous breakdown and passed away at the state mental hospital in Elgin, Illinois on August 29, 1904. He was sixty years old at the time.

Appendix B

The Family of Joseph Smith Sr. and Lucy Mack Smith

1. **Daughter Smith.** The first born child of Joseph Sr. and Lucy is simply recorded as: Daughter Smith, born about 1797 in Turnbrige, Orange County, Vermont.

2. **Alvin.** Born February 11, 1798 and died at the age of 25, November 19, 1823. Joseph received a special revelation concerning this brother whom he saw in the Celestial Kingdom, January 21, 1836. *(Pearl of Great Price)*

3. **Hyrum.** Hyrum was five years older than Joseph. He was born on February 9, 1800 and was killed with his brother in the Carthage Jail, June 27, 1844.

4. **Sophronia.** Born May 16, 1803. She married Calvin Stoddard who, though he believed in the restoration was excommunicated from the church twice. Two daughters were born to this union, one died in infancy.

   Calvin Stoddard died September 7, 1836. Sophronia later married William McCleary. They had no children. Sophoronia's second husband also preceded her in death. She died in 1876 and has no living descendants.

5. **Joseph Smith Jr.** It is interesting, as Cecil McGavin points out, that it is an American custom to give the first-born the father's name, but in this case it was given to the third son, "that prophecy might be fulfilled."

6. **Samuel Harrison.** Born March 13, 1808 and died July 30, 1844. Samuel married Mary Bailey. They had three daughters and one son. Mary died and he married Levira Clark who gave him three daughters.

   It will be remembered that Samuel had gone to help his brothers in the Carthage jail when he was recognized as a Smith. He was hurt as he raced from his would-be captors and never recovered. He died just a month and three days after Joseph and Hyrum.

   After Samuel's death his wife took her three daughters and

"some of Samuel's children by his first wife" to Utah where they were very active in the Utah Church.

7.   **Ephraim.** Born March 13, 1810 and died eleven days later, March 24, 1810.

8.   **William.** Born March 13, 1811 and died November 13, 1893. William had three wives and eight children. Caroline Amanda Grant had two daughters. Roxy Ann Grant, a sister of Caroline, gave him one son and one daughter. Eliza Sanborn bore him three sons and one daughter.

William had served as a member of the Quorum of the Twelve Apostles, but was excommunicated from the Church in October 1845 for "unchristian conduct." He was the only living brother of the Prophet Joseph at the time.

William's youngest son, Edson Don Carlos joined the Utah Church when he was seventy years old. He went West where he was an active faithful member. He died in 1939.

William spent the last years of his life in Elkader, Iowa where he died November 13, 1893. His headstone refers to him as "The Reverend William Smith."

9.   **Catherine.** Born July 12, 1812. She married Wilkens Jenkins Salisbury. He was "expelled from the Church in 1834 for intemperance." Four girls and four boys were born to this couple.

Cecil McGavin says, "For many years after the martyrdom and exodus from Nauvoo, the families of the prophet's three sisters, William's family, and others who remained on the Illinois prairie near Carthage or even in Nauvoo, became very silent on the subject of religion.

None of the Smiths who remained in Illinois joined any of the local churches until fifteen years after the Reorganized Church was started . . ."

Catherine was only forty years old when her husband died. "She spent forty-seven lonely years as a widow." She passed away February 1, 1900.

10.   **Don Carlos.** He was born March 15, 1813. He married Agnes Coolbirth. They had two daughters when Don Carlos died in Nauvoo on August 7, 1841.

Agnes was confused about going West. She said, "I feel alone, all alone. If there was a Carlos, or Joseph or Hyrum then how quickly I would be there."

Agnes remained in Nauvoo and later married William Pickett. Two sons were born to this couple. They later went to California but kept secret their connection with the Smiths. They did not affiliate with any church.

It is reported that Orrin Porter Rockwell met Agnes while he was visiting in California and found she had lost all of her hair. Porter said, "Few men did I love as I loved Don Carlos, and it will never be said of me that I passed up an opportunity to do his widow a favor."

Porter never cut his hair because he said that Joseph once told him that "as long as he wore his hair long, no enemy would ever have power over him."

However, seeing Agnes bald, he went to a barber shop, had his haircut and made into a wig for her.

11. **Lucy.** Born July 18, 1821 and died December 9, 1882.

Lucy married Arthur Millikin in 1840. Joseph performed the ceremony. Four sons and five daughters were born to this couple. The whole family became members of the Reorganized Church.

Acknowledgements

E. Cecil McGavin has done excellent research concerning the family of Joseph Smith in his books:

Nauvoo the Beautiful
Stevens and Wallis, Inc.
Salt Lake City, Utah (1946)

The Family of Joseph Smith
Bookcraft, Inc.
Salt Lake City, Utah (1963)

Much of the information concerning Emma is taken from these two books.

Other sources referred to:

History of the Church, Vol. VI
Compiled by B. H. Roberts
Deseret News Press
Salt Lake City, Utah

The Restored Church
William E. Barrett
Deseret Book Company
Salt Lake City, Utah

**A Comprehensive History of
The Church of Jesus Christ of
Latter-Day Saints. Vol. II**
B. H. Roberts
Deseret News Press
Salt Lake City, Utah (1930)

**Joseph Smith an American
  Prophet**
John Henry Evans
The Macmillan Company
New York (1940)

The Saints Herald
Independence, Missouri
Vol. 52, pages 386 and 484 (1905)
  86, page 939   (1939)
  62, page 1077   (1915)
  82, page 1519   (1935)

The Pearl of Great Price
Joseph Smith II
Church of Jesus Christ of
Latter-Day Saints
Salt Lake City, Utah

The Kingdom of God Restored
Carter Eldredge Grant
Deseret Book Company
Salt Lake City, Utah

Oliver Cowdery, Second
Elder and Scribe
Stanley R. Gunn
Bookcraft, Inc.
Salt Lake City, Utah

They Made Mormon History
Robert E. Day
Deseret Book Company
Salt Lake City, Utah (1973)

Blood Atonement and the Origin
 of Plural Marriage
Joseph F. Smith
Deseret News Press
Salt Lake City, Utah (1905)

Nightfall At Nauvoo
Samuel W. Taylor
Avon Books, 959 Eighth Avenue
New York, New York (1971)

**Nauvoo Kingdom on The
  Mississippi**
Robert Bruce Flanders
University of Illinois Press
Urbana, Illinois (1965)

**The History of the Reorganized
Church of Jesus Christ of Latter-
  Day Saints.   4 Vols.**
Lamoni, Iowa (1896-1903)

**Readings in L.D.S. Church History
  3 Vols.**
William E. Berrett and
  Alma D. Burton
Salt Lake City, Utah (1953-1959)

They Knew The Prophet
Hyrum & Helen Mae Andrus
Bookcraft, Inc.
Salt Lake City, Utah

About the Author

Erwin E. Wirkus

Erwin Wirkus was born in Germany and moved with his family to Idaho Falls, Idaho as a young boy. He served in the Northern States Mission and while there, participated in the 100th anniversary commemoration of the Prophet's martyrdom. He also served in the U.S. Army in the Pacific.

Since graduating from Utah State University in 1951, he has been teaching "release time" seminary for the Church. He is a former bishop and also served as president of the East Idaho Falls Stake for over eleven years. While presiding over the Austria Vienna Mission, he was called to organize the Iowa Des Moines Mission which included the Nauvoo, Illinois area. During his service there, organization of the Nauvoo Stake was approved to become the 1000th stake in the Church. He is currently serving as 2nd Counselor in the Idaho Pocatello Mission Presidency.

President Wirkus has served on the board of directors of the Idaho Falls LDS Hospital and has been chairman of the Lamanite Placement Program in Idaho. He and his lovely wife, Marie, are the parents of six children.